Newspaper Abstracts of CECIL AND HARFORD COUNTIES Maryland

1822-1830

F. Edward Wright

WILLOW BEND BOOKS
2008

WILLOW BEND BOOKS
AN IMPRINT OF HERITAGE BOOKS, INC.

Books, CDs, and more—Worldwide

For our listing of thousands of titles see our website at
www.HeritageBooks.com

Published 2008 by
HERITAGE BOOKS, INC.
Publishing Division
100 Railroad Ave. #104
Westminster, Maryland 21157

Copyright © 1984 F. Edward Wright

All rights reserved. No part of this book may be reproduced or transmitted in any form or by any means, electronic or mechanical, including photocopying, recording or by any information storage and retrieval system without written permission from the author, except for the inclusion of brief quotations in a review.

International Standard Book Numbers
Paperbound: 978-1-58549-075-2
Clothbound: 978-0-7884-7308-1

INTRODUCTION

For the most part, newspapers for Cecil and Harford Counties began in the 1820's. There was an earlier brief existence of the Abingdon Patriot in 1805 (see page 25). In 1820 the Bond of Union and Harford County Weekly Advertiser was founded in Bel Air. The Bond of Union was a Jackson paper. Opposition to Andrew Jackson brought about the establishment of a second newspaper in Bel Air, the Independent Citizen. Cecil County gave birth to its first newspaper in 1823 with the founding of the Elkton Press.

Many of the early copies of these newspapers can be found at the Library of Congress, Maryland Historical Society and Encoh Pratt Free Librry of Baltimore. I relied exclusively on these repositories for my source material.

Each numbered paragraph refers to a specific issue. On some occasions there was enough material to warrant two or more numbered paragraphs. Although the same item or information frequently appeared in consecutive issues a concerted effort was made to avoid repetitive items.

The specific source of the issue is shown by the trigraphs following the paragraph number as indicated below.

EPL - Elkton Press at the Library of Congress, Washingon, D. C.
EPM - Elkton Press at Maryland Historical Library, Baltimore
APL - Abingdon Patriot at the Library of Congress, Washington, D. C.
BUM - Bond of Union and Harford County Weekly Advertiser at the Maryland Historical Society, Baltimore
ICP - Independent Citizen at the Enoch Pratt Library, Baltimore

Hopefully the reader will find material herein which puts life into the times of his ancestors. Many of my earlier readers have found enjoyment in covering all the issues and fully immersing themselves in the past. I must warn you that the lists of names of persons with letters at the post office are fairly long and make up a significant portion of the book. I continue to feel that these lists can be helpful in establishing the existence of an individual in the community, as one might use tax lists, petitions, etc.

I have attempted to economize on space and include the maximum amount of information in this volume. Toward this end the following abbreviations have been used.

a. - acres
adj - adjoining
adm - administrator or administratrix of the estate of___
agnst - against
Balt - Baltimore
co - county
dau - daughter
decd - deceased
est - estate
exec - executor or executrix of a will
Harf - Harford
insol - insolvent

inst - instant (this month)
nr - near
occ - occupied
opp - opposite
Pa - Pennsylvania
pers - personal
p.m. - post master
p. o. - post office
prop - property
pt - part
res - residence or resided
Rev - Reverend
ult. - ultimate (last month)
yr(s) - year(years)

F. Edward Wright

1. EPL Feb 14 1824/Farm in Octorara Hundred adj lands of John Conrad, Elizabeth Walker, Mrs. Grubb and others with 2 good tenant houses, 1/2 mile from Conowingo Bridge Village, 1 mile from Baldfrier Ferry and 1 mile from Catholic Church; apply to James C. M'Dowell or Andrew R. Porter nr the premises/Teacher wanted for English School nr North East(?)/William Miller jr, Head of Sassafras, requests settlement of accounts agnst est of Frederick G. Briscoe, Kent Co, decd/Sale of tract in accordance with will of John Hammond Cromwell, Cecil Co, decd - Samuel Rowland, exec/Distillery for sale - John M'Cord, Elkton/Meliscent Abbott, Cecil Co exec of William F. Abbott, Cecil Co/James Morgan, George Beasten and Ambrose Price exec of James Morgan, sen, Cecil Co/Michel Montgomery, Cecil Co, adm of Thomas Montgomery, Cecil Co/Joel Reynolds, Cecil Co, adm of Richard Reynolds, Cecil Co/Hannah Crouch, Cecil Co, exec of Robert Crouch, Cecil Co/John Wroth, Cecil Co, adm of John Coppin, Cecil Co/John Janney, Cecil Co, adm of Isaac Tyson, Cecil Co/Samuel Ramsey, Cecil Co, exec of Andrew Ramsey, Cecil Co/Jane Patterson, William Patterson, adm of William Callender, Cecil Co/William Tylor, Cecil Co, adm of James Wallace, Cecil Co

2. EPL Feb 14 1824/John Wroth, Cecil Co, adm of Hance Severson, Cecil Co/John M'Cord, Elkton will rent his tavern, sign of the Wagon, together with 50 acres in Bart township between Strasburg and Wilmington, Lancaster Co, Pa; apply to James Andrews nr the premises or to John M'Cord/Rent - White house opp Mr. Lusby's tavern, occ by H. Stump as an office - Levi H. Evans/For rent - oil mill, bark mill, saw mill, nr Octoraro Bridge, part in Lancaster Co and part in Chester Co, Pa - James Andrews/House for rent now in possession of Thomas Biddle; also the farm; apply to Benjamin Pearce or Collins Tatman nr Elkton or Elizabeth Pearce (subscriber) res at Samuel Kerr's in Kent Co/For rent - tavern house in west end of Elkton occ by John and Isaac Wilson - Henry Bennett Jr/New fall goods - Rochester and Howard/For rent - three valuable fisheries at Turkey Point - Samuel Thomas, Turkey Point/Rowland Ellis seeks to hire cook and washer/Died at Chester-Town Wed 4 inst, William Brown, aged 54, afflicted with asthmatical and dropsical disease. In early life he enlisted in the cause of his country; a sterling Republican/Store house for rent on west end of Elkton occ by Isaac Wilson - John Kean/Store house for rent occ by Messrs Virtue and Hogg, two doors down from Mr. Peacock's Inn - Alexander Scott

3. EPL Feb 14 1824/For rent on Big Elk Creek, North Milford Hundred, known as Harmony Cotton Factory, 60 acres with large Factory House and Saw Mill, dwelling house and a number of tenant houses - William Cowan, Cowantown (5 miles from Elkton)/Benoni Veazey, Cecil Co, forwarns persons from taking assignment of a note payable to Edward Oldham jr of New Castle Co, Del/ Commission appointed to divide or appraise real est of Alexander Fulton - John M'Cockle, James C. M'Cowell, Jonas Preston, William Preston, Edmund Physick/ John T. Hart candidate for sheriff, Kent Co, in opposition to James Salisbury/ Cecil Co Chancery case - Jane Kidd vs Robert Love. Creditors of Robert Love request to exhibit claims of James Sewall, Register Chancery side of Cecil Court - Henry Hollngsworth, auditor by order of Hon. Richard T. Earle, Chancellor/Sheriff's sale at Port Deposit: (1) lot at Rock Run where Samuel Kerr res; (2) island near Rock Run; The late Mr. Burr stated that 2 excellent seats for mills or factories might be had on this land; (3) tract adj lands of John Patterson; (4) lot with 2 dwelling houes of which occ by David White for a number of years; (5) Fishery 1 miles below Octoraro nr Mrs. M'Elearys; and other prop of Samuel and Robert Kerr - Francis Gillespie, Sheriff

4. EPL Feb 14 1824/Sheriff's sale of tract on Bohemia Manor known as Court House Point, prop of Charles Oldham/Sale of farm and mill seat in Octoraro Hundred, adj lands of Francis Smith, Andrew Dunbar, and others, formerly site of "Husband's mill" - John Conrad, agent for heirs of J. Conrad, decd/Trustee's sale obtained by heirs of Samuel Miller, decd, reversionary interest of William C Miller and Deborah Miller and other heirs of Samuel Miller to real est devised by Samuel Miller to William, Deborah and John M. Miller during their lives and the fee simple in possession of that part devised to his son, James Miller, decd, the tracts, Consent, Stedman's Delight, Mill Privilege, including a grist mill (on Mill Pivilege) - Stevenson Archer trustee/Sale in accordance with the will of Robert Love, Cecil Co: plantation adj Susquehanna Canal - Thomas Fulton/Fruit trees - order through Zebulon Beasten, Elkton, or Dr G. S. Townsend, Brick Meeting House, Cecil Co/By order of Orphans Court, New Castle Co - sale of tract in Pencader Hundred, including mercant mill and saw mill, formerly known as Fisher's Mill, est of Jacob Tyson, decd - Abraham Egbert adm - Mathew Kean, Clerk, Orphans Court. Sale to be held at house of John Herdman, Innkeeper, New Ark/Sale in accordance with the will of William Howard: 2 lots called Prospect Hill, 3 miles from Elkton, 1 in the tenure of John H. Davidson (dwelling house, wagon makers and blacksmith shops) and second lot consists of 1 acre and dwelling house - Thomas Howard, Alexander Scott, exec/ White House for rent, Chestertown - George W. Thomas, Chestertown

5. EPL Mar 6 1824/for rent - brick house occ by Mr. Yates - Joseph Richardson, Elkton/Sale at house of Major Wigdon, Chesapeake, Cecil Co: frame building, res of John Stump, 530 feet from ferry house and tavern, occ by Major Wigdon - by order of Post Master Gen., U. S. - J. P. B...postmaster, Havre de Grace/ Sheriff's sale of dwelling house in Elkton next door to tavern occ by Mr. Peacock and where William H. Ward formerly res, prop of Louis Price, to satisfy debt due Robert C. Lusby and Elizabeth his wife, for the use of Francis Gillespie, use of James Sewall/For rent - store house adj Elkton Bank - John Partridge/Sheriff's sale of land 2 miles from Elkton of Joseph Thomas jr to satisfy debt due James Sewall/Sheriff's sale of land in Charlestown district, prop of Samuel M'Cullough and Robert Logan, at suit of James and Robert Cameron /Sale of store house and joiner shop formerly occ by Mr. Wolf and lately by Mr. Sergeant in Elkton - Israel Reynolds, Rising Sun, Summerhill/Sale of 5 shares of stock in Elkton Bank of Md - Apply to P. Harding, cashier or subscriber, John W. Comegys, nr Cecilton/Horse stolen from Moses Scott nr Elkton from store of William Cowan in Cowantown/For rent - farm called Mountain Farm, 150 acres of cleared land; apply to Thomas S. Thomas or Johnson Simpers or subscriber, Henry C. Ramsey, Balt/Fredus Price, Cecil Co, adm of Benjamin Price, Cecil Co/Thomas Huggins, Cecil Co, adm of John Conway, Cecil Co/Bennedict Craddock, Cecil Co, adm of Peregrine Stanley, Cecil Co/Elijah Eliason, Cecil Co, adm of Gertrude Craig, Cecil Co/William Manley, Cecil Co, adm of Sarah Manley, Cecil Co/Anne Coale, John Jewett, Cecil Co, exec of Skipwith Coale, Cecil Co/William Worthington, Cecil Co, adm of Zenas Worthington, Cecil Co

6. EPL Jun 12 1824/Letitia Davidson, Cecil Co, exec of William Davidson, Cecil Co/Sarah Turner, Cecil Co, exec of George C. Turner, Cecil Co/Benjamin W. Harris, Cecil Co, adm of William Whitham, Cecil Co/William Matthews, Cecil Co, adm of Frisby Wallace, Cecil Co/William Wingate, Cecil Co, adm of Edward Wingate, Cecil Co/Mary Moore, Cecil Co, adm of George Moore, Cecil Co/Margaret Brown, Cecil Co, exec of John Brown, Cecil Co/Margaret Burts, Ira Emmons, adm of Thomas Burts, Cecil Co/Cyrus Oldham, Cecil Co, adm of Israel White, Cecil Co/Regimental orders to fill vacancies in militia companies of 49th Regiment -

-2-

Robert C. Lusby, adj't/Dry goods - John N. Black, Charlestown/For sale - farm nr Rock Meeting House occ by Mary Wallaston, 21 acres, at Blue Bull tavern - David Mackey, trustee. Alexander Alexander will shew the prop/Samuel Downing offers reward for horse stolen from Downing's mill, Bart township, Lancaster Co/Sale of 300 acres of land, late the prop of George H. Kerr, decd, adj Cecil Furnace lands - Christopher Little, Francis Owens, agents for heirs of George H. Kerr/Shoe store, No. 5 Ricketts Row - William H. Hamer, agent

7. EPL Jun 12 1824/James Chamberlin & son have commenced boot & shoe manufactory in Elkton, opp Mr. Peackock's Inn/Married Thurs 3 inst by Rev Chambers, Andrew Armstrong to Miss Margaret Veach, both of New Castle Del/"Friends of General Jackson" invited to attend dinner at house of George Braddock's/"Friends of John Quincy Adams" invited to Mr. Beaston's Hotel/Federal Republicans invited to a dinner at Washington Hotel in Elkton/Clover Hay - Charles Miller, Little Elk/Lumber for sale - Francis Gottier, Elkton/Horse missing - Samuel Miller/ Horse missing - Jesse Thomas nr Elkton/Dry goods - W. Wingate, North East/ George Churchman exec of George Churchman, decd, East Nottingham Hundred/Thomas Peacock, Chestertown warns agnst receiving bond given by him to Gilbert Christfield .. in satisfaction of debts due by him to certain Charles Johns, since endorsed for the use of Gersham W. Lambert/Samuel A. Miller requests settlement of accounts/Lumber for sale - Enoch Cloud, Elkton/Drug and medicine store - Caleb Parker/Davidson D. Pearce reports stray mare/Farm for sale where he res nr Rock Run - John Patterson/Sheriff's sale of tract below Frenchtown, prop of Thomas Foster, to satisfy debt due Pollard Owens/Sheriff's sale of interest of Thomas Biddle to 300 acres in Back Creek Neck to satisfy debt due to Thomas Jones/Sheriff's sale of tract called Plumb Point in Elk Neck, prop of John Wingate to satisfy claim of Mary Wilson and Nicholas Hyland adm of Alexander Wilson/Sheriff's sale of interest of Caleb Edmondson to tracts nr Brick Meeting House/Dry goods - George Kidd, nr Port Deposit/Mare mising - John Hurlock nr Georgetown Cross Roads/Tailoring business - Benjamin W. Hazlop, Charlestown, having removed from Balt

8. EPL Nov 13 1824/Daniel Job, Cecil Co, exec of Margaret White, Cecil Co/Benjamin Benson - coach and harness maker, Smyrna, Del/Chair manufactory - Robert Burchall, Elkton, nr James Pugh's tavern/Cabinet manufactory - Dunbar and Foster, next door to Mr. Burchall/Manufacture of Piano Fortes commenced by John H. Pennington, Smyrna, Del/Negroes for sale - Ambrose M. Price/Candle manufactory recommenced by Samuel R. Hogg at his store/Samuel Miller, Elkton, having met with a serious loss last spring, requests payment of debts/Sale of farm nr Chestertown - Samuel Covington/Archibald Gordon, New Castle Co, Del, Samuel M'Intire, adm of Thomas Vail, New Castle Co, Del/Commission to divide real est in Elkton of John Springer, decd, Cecil Co - Frisby Henderson, Alexander Scott, Adam Whann, Joshua Richardson, Thomas Howard/Farm for sale where he lives adj Elkton - Henry Andrews/Plough & harrow stolen - James Sewall, Elkton/More new goods - John F. Cazier, North East/...(portion of this issue is missing...)

9. EPL Sep 1 1827/Jacob M. Taylor and Edward Wilson, Cecil Co, exec of Isaac Taylor, Cecil Co/Hezekiah Foard, Cecil Co, adm of Andrew Foard, Cecil Co/Joseph W. Miller, Cecil Co, adm of William Miller, Cecil Co/Edward Wilson, Cecil Co, adm of Jeremiah Taylor, Cecil/John Wroth, Cecil Co, adm of Catharine Price, Cecil Co and John B. Price, Cecil Co/Nathan Hilles nr Rising Sun, seeks apprentice to tanning business/Jacob M. Taylor, Cecil Co, exec of Margaret Ratliff, Cecil Co/Anne Price, Samuel H. Freeman, Cecil Co, adm of William Price, Cecil Co/Daniel M. Cooley, Cecil Co, adm of John Cooley, Cecil

-3-

Co/Robert Archibald, Cecil Co, adm of John Cooley, Cecil Co/William D. Jenks requests debts due him be paid to R. C. Lusby/Trustee's sale in a cause wherein Thomas Garret was the complainant and Dennis Doughterty and others were respondents: tracts, Alexander's Lot and Strabane; also tract formerly granted to Joseph Watkins and Samuel Davis; also land purchased by Thomas Garret of Thomas Wagner as described in mortgage from James Collins and Jared Chesnut to Thomas Garret; includes Woollen Factory on Christiana Creek, N. Milford Hundred, Cecil Co, 500 yards from where location of City of Washington was fixed - Tobias Rudulph, trustee

10. EPL Sep 1 1827/Sheriff's sale of right of Jonathan Albertson in East Nottingham adj lands of Moses Gillingham/Sheriff's sale of house nr William Coal's Tavern, prop of Thomas Huggins, to satisfy debt due Havre de Grace Bank/Sheriff's sale of house in Elkton, south side of Main St and 20 acres adj land of William and David Rickets, 1 mile from Elkton, to satisfy debts due to Israel Reynolds/Zeb Rudulph inspector of weights and measures, Cecil Co/Sale of woodland in neighborhood of Egg Hill adj lands of Elkton Forge Com. Apply to Daniel M'Cauley or William M'Clay - J. Beard and heirs of Hugh Beard/John C. Groome advertises that debts due John G. Ruan will be put in hands of a collector/Zebulon C. Austin, James O. Austin, adm of James Austin, New Castle Co, Del/Sarah Lee, nr Frenchtown, reports stray dark red cow/William Thompson exec of James Thompson to sell tavern in Pencader Hundred, New Castle Co, Del/ Farm for rent at Black's Cross Roads in Kent Co belonging to Mrs. A. B Hollingsworth, now in tenure of Col. George Spry - J. C. Groome/George Duffield, Henry Duffield, Munster mills, adm of George Duffield, decd/Ephraim Sterling, Cecil Co, adm of Catharine Ann Mansfield, Cecil Co/Henry Southern, at Chesapeake and Delaware Canal, nr Buck-tavern, offers reward for missing horse

11. EPL Sep 1 1827/Extracts from the minutes and Proceedings of the Levy Court for the year of 1827 - Collectors: John V. Price, 1st dist; Edward Wilson, 2nd dist; John E. Simpers, 3d dist; James Gerry, 4th dist - Inspector of Weights and Measures: Zebulon Rudulph - Constables: 1st dist: John Manlove, Joshua S. Hudson, John Rawlings, William Hackett; 2nd dist: Thomas Miller, William Maclay, Samuel Wilson, Evan D. Yates, Andrew Hall, Richard Boulden, John Stanton; 3rd dist: Thomas Burns, Eli Janney, Azarias Penington, John Jannings, John E. Simpers, 4th dist: John A. Begley, John D. M'Cutchen, James H. Brickley, Jacob Williams, Samuel Beaty(?), Tobias R. Biddle, Joshua H. Dorsey, John H. Porter, Charles A. Newland - Trustees of the Poor: Theodore Thomas, Charles T. Foard, William Kirk Clothier, Benjamin F. Mackall and Eben'zr Wherry - Judges: 1st election dist: George Beaston, William Morgan and Joseph Hanson; 2nd election dist: Nicholas Hyland (of Ed.), Andrew F. Henderson and John Evans (of John); 3rd election dist: John N. Black, Robert Cameron and John Mauldin; 4th election dist: John Briscoe, Elias Penington and Thomas L. Savin - James Sewall, Clk/Joseph Redue candidate for sheriff, Kent Co

12. EPL Sep 1 1827/For sale - Grist and Saw mills, situated at head of Morgan's creek, Kent Co, Md; grist mill has been well repaired in the improved plan of cast iron cog wheels, working into a very large spur wheel; and every part of the running gears, water wheel, and great frame, or husk, as it is called, has been made entirely new within a few months past and also, pier head or forebay, bolting cloth and gears are new and of the best quality; grain is at this very dry season sent to her from 15 to 20 miles. The Saw Mill is in very good order and can by very profitably employed until a drought prevails. The dam and flood gates are in good order. A tolerable good dwelling house with other out houses are on the premises - James Hanson/Isaiah

Cooper, 4th dist; John W. Thomas, Charles Town Dist; John Ross; and Dr. Granville S. Townsend, 4th dist, candidates for Md legislature/Thomas McCreary and Lilburn Price, candidates for sheriff, Cecil Co/William Mackey candidate for Gen. Assembly

13. EPL Jul 19 1828/Rev Cole will preach at Court House in Elkton Sun next/ Sheriff's sale of tract of Jonathan Albertson in east Nottingham nr Rogers' Mill, to satisfy debt due Isaac Reynolds/Mare missing - John Stanton/W. Wingate, cash'r Elkton Bank of Md, announces meeting of stock holders/Joseph B. Sims, Cantwell's Bridge, New Castle Co, Del, offers reward for George Anderson, negro, 21-22, middle size, large eyes/Camp meeting to be held in Mr. Lecount's woods, Middletown, Del/Henry Jamar, Elkton, seeks to employ apprentice to black smith's business/Sale at Cornelius Smith's tavern, Port Deposit: real est of Mrs. Sarah Thomas, adj Port-Deposit, called Anchor & Hope, on which William Orr occ one portion as one of two farms - Washington Hall, Henry Chamberlaine, Thomas White, commissioners/Families wanted for Endeavor Cotton Factory nr Stanton Del - Joseph Mendenhall, on the premises/Philip Wilson Jr, Cecil Co, exec of Philip Wilson, Cecil Co/Thomas John Slicer, Cecil Co, exec of John Slicer, Cecil Co/Packet Boat from St. Georges - T. Mulford/Isaiah Cooper, and James Hart, Cecil co, insol debtors, to be discharged from confinement/David Gilmore, Cecil Co, adm of Capt Samuel Gilmore, Cecil Co

14. EPL Jul 19 1828/Furniture for sale - Sarah P. Sullivan, Elkton/Joseph Townsend, Balt City, Jeremiah Brown, Slater Brown of Little Britain Co, exec of Joseph England, Cecil Co/Elisha Kirk, John Marshall, Cecil Co, exec of Doctor James Beard, Cecil Co/John Sharpley, Cecil Co, adm of Thomas Pryor, Cecil Co/ Thomas White, Cyrus Oldham, Cecil co, adm of James Gillespie, Cecil Co/ George R. Howard, Cecil Co, adm of Samuel Bowser, Cecil Co/Wool carding at his mills, 7 miles above Elkton, will be rec'd at Messrs Wingate & Manly, Elkton; Benjamin W. Harris, Back Creek; Alfred C. Nowland, Cecilton - William Garett/ Thomas Janney, Cecil Co, adm of James Janney, Cecil Co/George Biddle, Cecil Co, adm of Peregrine Biddle, Cecil Co/Sarah Gilmore, Ira Emmons, Cecil Co, exec of Capt David Gilmore, Cecil Co/Commission to partition real est of Jacob Johnston - Thomas Howard, Benjamin F. Mackall, Thomas Moore, Joshua Richardson, Amos A. Evans, Elkton/Sale of plantation in West Nottingham Hundred, former res of Jacob Haines, 80 acres, log dwelling house, 2 stories high, stone spring house, large frame barn with celler - William Brown, Moses Moore, Immer Knight/Negro woman for sale - William Hogg, nr Charlestown/Mill seat and farm for sale in East Nottingham; apply to Joseph Harlan nr the premises or Joseph G. Partridge, Balt/William Rochester, having been in business 5 yrs, requests settlement of accounts/Camp meeting for Port Deposit station in Mr. D. Magredy's woods

15. EPL Jul 19 1828/Letters remaining at P.O., Elkton, July 1 1828:Samuel C. Allston; Andrew Alexander; Ruth Ash; William Black; John Biddle; Noble Biddle; Mary Boram; Henry Baker; Nancy Crage; Mary E. H. Clayton; Jesse Chick; Jacob, John or Philip Clyme; James Valingtine; Lydia Deal; Joshua H. Dorsey; Thomas Fox; Susannah Farra; Jonathan Greenwood; Thomas Gilbert; John Groome; Lydia Gordon; Joseph Gilpin; Benjamin Hyland; Lambert G. Hyland; William or George Hutcheson; Sarah Huxulis; Thomas Hinds; Caleb Harper; William Hewitt; John Jordon; Samuel Irwin; Ann C. Jackson; Sarah Lewis; Andrew Lyarson; John Marshall; John M'Cord; Ann M'Caslin; Thomas Mullit; Jacob Mackey; Jane Moore; Margaret M'Kinley; Robert J. Musgrave; Sylvester Nugent; William Nicholson; Henry Norman; Emily Oldham; Charles Oldham; P. Harding; O. C. Pryce; Ann Price; Matthew Pearce; Thomas Parker; James Rider; Thomas Rowe; William

Radcliffe; Tobias Rudulph; Ephraim Robinson; Mary Rossell; William Richardson; John Stanton; David S. Sharp; Mary Simpson; Robert Sergant; Theodore Thomas; Ann Thomas; William M. Townsand; Samuel Thomas; Samuel Walker; Grace Worrell; Samuel Wilson; William H. Wilson; John Waton - Adam Whann, P.M.

16. EPL Jul 26 1828/Dr. J. H. Scott offers his services at Charlestown/Thomas Howard sen. offers reward for apprentice to wheelwright and blacksmith business - William H. Wilson/Letters remaining at P.O., Port Deposit: Miss Hannah Allen; William Allen; William Akins; Jacob Bromwell; John Cochran; Capt Rendel Coochlen; Dinah Cox; William Dickerman; William D. Jenks; James H. East; Thompson Graham c/o Cornelius Smith; William Jones c/o Mr. Wall; Lorenza D. Morgan, schooner William & Eliza; Edmund Physick; Sterrett & Walker; Shaffer; Capt. Hiram Woolford on board schooner New Castle; Doct. James Warden c/o Mr. Smith, Innkeeper - Samuel Nesbitt jr, P.M./Thomas Howard, has taken store formerly occ by Levi H. Evans/Lots for sale - John Creswell

17. EPL Aug 2 1828/Died in this town Mon last, 28 ult, Mrs. Maria Stanton, wife of John Stanton, aged 38/Sale at Rowland Ellis's Tavern in Elkton: interest of James B. Wallace, decd (as one of the devisees of his father, Dr. George Wallace): tracts, Wallace's Good Design, New Hall, Addition to New Hall, Ricketts' Triangle, Zebulon's Fancy, being same farm whereon Andrew Stalcup res/Dissolution of partnership of Justus Dunbar and Robert Virtue/Edmund Physick, Cecil Co, exec of Henry W. Physick, Cecil Co/Nicholas Hyland, Cecil Co, adm of Reese Crooshanks, Cecil Co/Edward Wilson, Cecil exec of Jacob Egner, Cecil Co/Jesse Boulden, Cecil Co, exec of Richard Boulden, Cecil Co/Committed to Cecil Co jail, negro man, about 26, 5 ft 9 inch, stout, calls himself John Brown; says he was brought up nr Bucks Co by a Mr. Disborough and that his parents are free; he has been employed 12 months as a hand on a small packet, Balt to Port Deposit - Thomas Miller Jr, Cecil Co

18. EPL Aug 16 1828/Sheriff's sale of interest of Leonard Krouss: tract, West Nottingham adj lands of Charles Harris, 37 acres, for debt due Elkton Bank/ Cabinet maker - Justus Dunbar, at former stand of Dunbar & Virtue/Cabinet maker - Robert Virtue/A race at Havre de Grace - Hall & Huggins/Sheriff's sale of tract in Back Creek Neck adj lands of Benjamin Pearce, heirs of Jeremiah Taylor and others, known as Hisponilia, prop of Richard F. Alexander, to satisfy debt due Mary Nowland, surviving exec of Edward Ford/Sheriff's sale of farm, 2 tracts, named Abraham Choice and New Garden, in Sassafras Neck adj lands of Samuel Ruly, Col. Veazey, and others, formerly owned by Joseph Stockton, decd, prop of Sarah & Eliza Davis, to satisfy debts of William Wingate adm of Edward Wingate & Isaac Price/Robert Alexander, Cecil Co, reports stray colt trespassing on the enclousres of Thomas & William Cockran (Robert Alexander living with Thomas and William Cockran) - William Mackey, Justice of Peace/Sheriff's sale of title of William R. Pearce to farm, part of Pearce's Neck, 990 acres, in Sassafras Neck/Companies of 49th Regiment to muster on the Old Field opp William Polk's stone store house nr the canal

19. EPL Aug 16 1828/Sheriff's sale of claim of Hyland Price to tract in Nottingham at suit of state, use of John W. Etherington and wife, use of Dinsmore & Kyle/ Sheriff's sale at house of Fredus Price, 500 acres of land, at suits of John Reynolds, Enoch Levering, and Jesse Levering, endorsers of George Beaston/ Sheriff's sale at house of Hozea Terry: right of said Terry, 30 acres, adj lands of Abel Mearns, John C. Cameron, and others/Sheriff's sale of interest of Samuel Gilmore to house in Port Deposit at suit of John Edmondson/Sheriff's sale of intrest of James Hamilton: tract, Montgomery adj lands of Stephen Woodrow and others; also fishery adj lands of Urban Holiday,

at suit of Samuel Graham, use of James Gerry/Sherif's sale at house of Barney Mullen, title of Barney Mullen and Elizabeth his wife, to house in Elkton, at suits of Robert, John and William Wingate

20. EPL Aug 23 1828/Sale of pers prop of Theodore Thomas, decd, nr Elkton - Stevens W. Woolford, adm

21. EPL Aug 30 1828/Married Thurs 21 by Rev James Magraw, Andrew Brickley of Brickley town to Miss Mary Campbell of the Rising Sun/Died at his res nr Elkton Sat last, Major John R. Evans, aged 57/Died in this town Wed last, Zebulon Beaston, aged 57/William Archibald seeks to employ journeymen carpenters, Port Deposit

22. EPL Sep 13 1828/Died in his res nr Elkton Thurs night last, Tobias Rudulph, in 42d yr; funeral this morning; citizens living on main st are requested to close windows and doors while the funeral is passing as a mark of respect/John M. Johnston, Cecil Co, adm of Rachel Ricketts, Cecil Co/Stevens W. Woolford, Cecil Co, adm of Theodore Thomas, Cecil Co/Sarah Jones, Cecil Co, adm of John Jones, Cecil Co/William Reynolds adm of Henry M. Hayes, Cecil Co/Joseph M'Coy, Cecil Co, adm of Eleanor Thomas, Cecil Co/Davidson D. Pearce, Cecil Co, adm of Jacob M. Taylor, Cecil Co

23. EPL Sep 20 1828/Died nr Newark, Sep 12, in 72d yr, Elizabeth Robeson of Newport Del, member of Meth Society since its infancy in Del/Died after a short illness morning of 11 inst, Green Hill, Cecil Co, where she had res upwards of 50 yrs, Ann Sheredine, aged nearly 70 (long obituary)/Sheriff's sale at house of Daniel Ramsey: undivided fourth part of farm now occ by Ramsey adj land of Robert Cristy in Nottingham, prop of Samuel Tyson, at suit of James Shearer and David Shearer/Commission to receive subscriptions to capitol stocks of a turnpike road, Port Deposit to Columbia Pa - Henry S. Stites, Cornelius Smith, Lewis Thomas, Alexander E. Grubb, James Gerry, Washington Hall, John Creswell/ Sale of plantation whereof William Stackhouse died, seized of 11 acres in New Munster, Cecil Co - James Jackson, trustee, Elk Forge

24. EPL Sep 27 1828/Examination of students of West-Nottingham Academy - James Magraw, Principal

25. EPL Oct 25 1828/William C. Scott - atty at law/Augustus Miller, atty at law, office opp Mr. Peacock's Inn/Account books stolen from Robert Carter, Cecil Paper mills/Nicholas Vandegrift forwarns persons from hunting on Welsh Point/Fishery, lately occ by William Ricketts, for rent on western side of Elk River where she res, Elizabeth Hyland adm of Jacob Hyland/Letters remaining at P.O., Port Deposit: Jehoackim Brickley c/o H. Stiles; Bing Campbell; Lawson Cooley c/o Neiper Gorrell; Andrew Dunn; Underwood Dann; James East; Ira Emmons; John Herney; Joshua Johnston; John Ludenum; Philip Lewis c/o Samuel Ford; Capt J. Moore; Capt R. Michel; Ann M'Cormick; Henry Norman c/o Mr. Crouce; Edmund Physick; Samuel Rexford; Jacob Stricker; B. H. Stevens; James H. Springer;Thomas Taylor; Thomas White; Orin Wells. - S. Nesbitt, P.M./Jacob Wallon will rent his house and farm, Back Creek, Cecil Co/Ann B. Hollingsworth offers reward for negro boy John/Robert H. Hays - Whereas my wife Eleanor Hays has eloped ...I am determined not to pay any debts.../Sale by decree of Circuit Court of U.S., The Rockland Estate, 2 miles from Port Deposit (detailed description). It will be shewn by J. W. Thomas or C. A. Thomas, res on the farm - Nath'l Williams, trustee

26. EPL Nov 1 1828/Teacher wanted, Head of Bohemia - William Crow, sen., John M. Flintham, Cyrus Tatman

27. EPL Nov 8 1828/Commission to value or divide lands held by Hyland Price, James Hyland Price, and heirs of Hugh Price which said James Hyland Price and Hugh Price are devisees of John Price, decd - William B. Biles, Samuel Marnes, Joseph Harlan, Cyrus Oldham, William Mackey

28. EPL Jul 11 1829/Died at Conawingo 20 Jun, Isaiah Brown in 57th yr/Died at Charlestown in this co 20 ult, Doctor Francis LeBaron, aged 46, formerly apothecary General U.S. Army/Dr. Caleb W. Cloud offers his services in dwelling lately occ by Dr. LeBaron, decd/Commission of Cecil Co to value and divide real est of Isaac Hall - John Mackey, Abraham D. Mitchell, Jacob Hylaman, William Mackey, William Fulton/Negroes for sale, prop of Howard Roach, decd: Sam 18, John 15, George 14, William 10, Jacob 8, Isaac 4, Francina 20, Margaret 12, Catherine 12, Jane 11, Abraham 8 - Henry Bennett adm of H. Roach/Letters remaining at P.O., Elkton, July 1 1929: Elizabeth Aux; Ann P. Boulden; William Barnett; George Bryan; Rachel Boulden; John Coldwell; James Cummings, sen; Jane Clark; William Crawford sen; Alex Craig; Mary Ann Chance; William Donaldson; Robert L. Ducket; Rev L. Epinett; Jonas Elias; David Evans; Thomas Fox; Josiah L. Foard; George M. Gill; Henry Hopkins; Thomas Janney; George Knight; D. L. Moore; Elizabeth Murphy; James Martin; Doct. William Miller; Mary Miller; Zebulon M'Kensey; James Mathews; Joseph W. Miller; Joseph Milles; Thomas M'Crery; Charles Oldham; John V. Price; Grace Robinson; Mary Reynolds; Washington Rice; James D. Rider; Henry Reynolds; William Simpers; Doct James Sykes; Gustin Stups; Edward Silleto; John Smith; John Spencer; Sarah Shields; Thomas Stradley; Saml Springer; Abraham Warum; Rachel Work; N. Wilkinson - Adam Whann, Post Master

29. EPL Jul 11 1829/Nathan Tyson, East Nottingham, Cecil Co, offers reward for indented girl, named Elizabeth Knitzburg, about 11(?) yrs of age/Mary Tyson advertises that Joseph Tyson, in the fall of 1827 eloped from her bed and board without just cause and forewarns persons from paying him any debts due her/Petition to sell and divide real est of Stephen H. Dorsey, Cecil Co, decd/Petition to sell and divide real est of William Mullen, decd, Cecil Co/Summer goods and groceries - Thomas Howard, Jr, Elkton/Cloverseed Mill at his res on Little Elk - Henry F. Mackall/Letters remaining at P.O. Cecilton: John W. Wirt; Jonathan Greenwood; John C. Murphey; John H. Price; John Anaudain; John Mittan; Lilburn Price; Miss Mary Eliason; Mrs. Ann Mercer; Mrs. Hezekiah Jones; Miss Mary Roberts; Mrs. E. H. Price; Mrs. Rebecca Ward; Christopher Jones; Benjamin Mercer; Ezekiel Stevenson; Stephen Moore; Squire Harris; Henry Hessey; David Miller; Zebulon Lusby; O. Horsey; Miss Ellen Lee - James Ford, p.m.

30. EPL Jul 11/Letters remaining at P.O., Port Deposit: Capt. Solomon Borton; Capt. Daniel Bacon; Mescus M. Badger; Richard Chany; William Cosgrove; Henry Dickerman; Ira Emmons; Ryer M. French; Mr. Hawkins; S. Hartshorn; Hiram Kimble, suger maker; Mr. Kenedy Innkeeper; John D. Lawlis; Solomon Miller col'd man; M. Nisbit; Edmund Physick; Adriana Physic; Elizabeth Physick; Mr. Philips; S. Reynolds jr; Francis Sugars; Benjamin H. Stevens; Isreal Smith; George Senney; George H. Turner; Sarah Vogdes; Levi Vosbury - S. Nesbitt Jr, p.m./Dr. A. M. Freeman, dentist, Wilmington, at No. 66 Shipley St/Sheriff's sale of tract south side of Bohemia river adj lands of heirs of late Peregrine Biddle occ by John V. Price, 50 acres, prop of William D. Mercer, to satisfy debts due to Samuel and William Meteer/Sale of farm in West Nottingham, 100

-8-

acres, occ by Mr. Irwin - Abner Taylor, livng at Samuel Taylor's nr the premises/John W. Maffit, North East, has taken mill known as Maffit's Mill/Marshal Ney to be let to mares - Samuel Hollingsworth, Elkton

31. EPL Sep 12 1829/Stray cow to farm of subscriber, 1 mile from North-East - Thomas Russell/George Jones offers reward for apprentice boy John H. Eliason, about 18/Sale of colored boy - James Ray, Philip's mills, nr Newark Del/ Sheriff's sale of right of Fredus Price to tract occ by Edward Pennington, 500 acres/Sheriff's sale of right of Barny Mullin and Elizabeth his wife, formerly Elizabeth Barnes: lot in Elkton of 1/2 acre/Sheriff's sale at house of John and Samuel Severson: claim of John Severson to land where John Severson res, consisting of 200 acres, prop of John Severson and Thomas Severson, decd/49th Regiment to assembly for inspection and drill at Cheek's Old Field - John N. Black, Brig. Insp./Races - A. C. Smith, between Head of Sassafras and village of Warwick/Dry goods - Thomas Hayward Jr/Lee's anti bilious Pills - Thomas Roach & Co, Elkton/Sheriff's sale at Mrs. Owens: all Samuel McKowen's right to house occ by him in Charlestown at suit of Thomas Sturgeon/Sheriff's sale of right of John M'Collough to house in Port Deposit at suit of Francis Gordon/ Sale of small farm of 70 acres in East Nottingham on road from Rogers' Mill to Brick Meeting House. Prop will be shewn by Joseph Thomas res on premises - Thomas Miner

32. EPL Sep 12 1829/Joseph Stoops offers reward for apprentice to blacksmithing business, George Ball/For rent - Tavern occ by James Gallaway at the Tide Lock of the Susquehanna Canal - John W. Thomas, manager for Susquehanna Canal Co/ James Mathews, west Elkton, seeks to employ Journeyman weavers/John Rarrick seeks apprentice to carpentering business/Chancery sale in cause of Martha Poag, complainant; Jesse, Thomas, and Elizabeth McCreery, John Poag and others were defendants of prop, mortgaged by William McCreery to Samuel Poag on Little Elk Creek: tract, Consent and Chambers Venture (2-story log dwelling)/ Commission to sell and divide real est of Stephen Hayes - Benjamin F. Mackall, James Jackson, Edward Wilson, Benjamn Bowen, John M. Johnson/Same commission as above to sell and divide real est of Stephen Paschell, Cecil Co/Sow and pigs taken up when trespassing - James Burgoyne living at Hollingsworth old mill/George Jones - tailor/Hugh Dougherty and son, tailors, Elkton, have removed to house lately occ by James Morrow opp res of Dr. John Groome/Patricus Finegan's Fashionable Tailoring Establishment, opp Mr. Peacock's Hotel, Elkton/New Hat manufactory at the house formerly occ by Mrs. Waggoner opp dwelling of Henry Hollingsworth - William H. Calvert/William W. Ramsay, Carpenter's Point, Cecil Co, offers reward for negro boys, Patrick, about 17, 5 ft 5-6 inch; and Henry about 16, 5 ft 5-6 inch/Several houses and farm for sale - William Ricketts, nr Elkton

33. EPL Sep 26 1829/Dry goods - William Rochester/Fall goods - Rudulph & Torbert/ Stray cow reported by Thomas Russell/Sale of farm in Cecil Co on Sassafras river called Silvanus Folly adj land of late Peregrine Ward 3d; Capt Mitchell res on prop - E. F. Chambers, trustee/Sale of farm in Sassafras Neck called Belhaven, late the prop of Thomas Stevens and formerly prop of Susan Stevens; George Price is tenant - E. F. Chambers, trustee/Samuel Fox, nr Church Hill, offers reward for mulatto man, about 23, about 5 ft 4-5 inch; he calls himself John Washington Reason; his wife got free a few days before he ran off; her name is Jane, about 18, manumitted by Mrs. Elizabeth Quimby or Sutton and served last of her time with William Foreman; Jane has a mother in Balt

34. EPL Oct 3 1829/Partnership of William Wingate and Charles K. Manly

dissolved/ Match race in the Old Mill Lane; horses owned by David Mackey and William Robinson - James Pugh/Public sale of farm, grist and saw-mill in Cecil Co, 3 1/2 miles from Brick Meeting House - apply to James Worth, on the premises/ Letters remaining at P.O. Elkton: Alexander & Morrow; Robert Allen, M.D.; Andrew Allison; John Porter Brown; Lambert Biddle; A. Bennett; John Creswell; W. Cooper, race rider; Mary Ann Cloward; W. B. Donaldson; Miss Eliza Evans; Edward L. Foard; William Gilpin; Hannah Gibbs; James Hudson; William Henris(?); William Hesson; Miss Sarah A. Harding; Rev H. N. Hatchkins; George Jameson jr; Miss Deborah Jones; Edward S. Keasby; James Long; John S. Mulow; Catharine Murdock; James Morrow; James G. Moore; A. D. Mitchell; James Mercer; John Marshall; Margaret Milburn; Charles M'Coy; Thomas Morgan; Sylvester Nugent; Edward Oldham; Miss Mary Porter; John Partridge; William Rochester; William Ricketts, cooper; Miss H. D. Rudolph; Jerry Short; Edward Short; Miss E. Stidlam; Watson Scarborough; James Scott, cartwright; John Scarborough; Robert Sergant; Robert Skinner; Emsen Tyson; Mr. Tremble; Michael Trump; Samuel Tibbitt; Dav E. Veazey; James Valentine; Sarah Vance; William Wright; Jane Williamson; Thos. White & Cyrus Oldham; William Ward; March Wesley - A. Whann, p.m./Trustee's sale in pursuance of general order of Balt Co Court in case of insolvent debtors, at store recently occ by Isaiah Cooper, in town of Conowingo/Assortment of dry goods, groceries, crockery-ware, medicines - George Gordon Belt, John Glenn

35. EPM JUL 5 1823/Died Sat 20 ult at the res of his brother-in-law, John M'Corkle in Nottingham Hundred, James P. Ewing of Octorara Hundred; funeral following day/Mary Craig adm of William Craig Jr/Richard Lockwood adm of John T. Cochran/Peter Bouchell adm of John Bouchell/Ambrose Price adm of Susan Hays/William Woodall adm of Melescent Bristow/Amos A. Evans and John Evans adm of John Evans/William Crow adm of John Crow/William Miller adm of John King/Andrew R. Porter adm of Eleanor Porter/Jacob Ash and Samuel Holland adm of Jacob Casho/Ambrose Price adm of David Mahr/William Miller adm of William Williams/Dry Goods - Samuel Miller, Elkton/George Jones, Tailor, 3 doors below Elkton Hotel/Dry Goods - Levi H. Evans/100,000 feet of white pine boards, 200,000 shingles - Enoch Cloud, Elkton/For Sale - prop lately occ by John Frey on Octorara Creek, forge and furnace - Jeremiah Cosden, trustee/Dissolution of partnership of Job Haines and James Carter, in the potting business (to be carried on under the firm of Haines & Greer)/George Hardy, tailor, opp Fountain Inn, Elkton/Penelope Wells offers reward for light sorrel horse stolen from her pasture on the Cherry Hill road about 2 1/2 miles from Elkton; supposed to have been stolen by a man calling himself Edward Davis, about 5 ft, 9-10 inches

36. EPM Jul 5 1823/Letters remaining at P.O. Elkton: Richard F. Alexander, Eleanor Anderson, John Black, William H. Barrot, Samuel Bohel, David Boyd, George H. Butler, John Beedle, Joseph Bryan, Albert G. Bryan, Rebecca Brown, Samuel R. Briscoe, Jeremiah Cosden, William Crawford, James Cochran, Charity Cazier, Catharine Dysart, William F. Dorsey, Leige Denning, Elizabeth Eliason, Jacob Egnor, James Ewing, Johna Evans, Moses Ely, Elizabeth Ford, John Gordon, Eliza Grindager, Henry Hayes, Nicholas Hyland, Henry Killen, George Kidd, Ann R. Kilgore, Joseph A. Miller, John Miller, James M'Gregor, James M'Ewen, William M'Cummins, Robert Moore, Archibald Nickle, William Orr, Mary A. Oldham, John Philips sen., Samuel Price, William C. Pennington, William Piner, Mary Robinson, Tobias Rudolph, Joseph Reed, William Sharp, John Short, Henry Simpson, Jesse Simpers, Samuel Spratt, William Stelling, James Scott, Jane Shearer, John Tealar, Haret Thomas, John Thompson, James Vance, Margaret Vandever, Union Lodge, W. M. 5; Joseph Wilcox, Mary Wilson Nath. Wolfe,

Margaret Walmsley, John Williamson, John Williams - Adam Whann, P.M.

37. EPM Jul 26 1823/Eleanor Lusby adm of William Lusby/Suicide of William Hood Jr of AA Co, about 40, by burning himself; left wife and 11 small children/Died in this town Wed last, Samuel T. Purnell, youngest son of James Purnell, in 10th yr of his age/Notice re Trustees of the Poor - William Ricketts, Treasurer/James Sewal, Clk, requests settlement of accts with Levy Court/Auction at house of Nathaniel Bender, Innkeeper, Brick Meeting House, Cecil Co: the stock of store goods (late of E. Kirk & son) - Timothy Kirk /Doctor Abraham Tillotson has commenced the practice of medicine and surgery at the former res of his father, the late Dr. Abraham Tillotson nr Elkton /Camp meeting in Merritt's woods/Elkton Hotel - Zebulon Beaston/Samuel Phillips exec of Thomas Lowe/James H. Brickley adm of Jehoiakim/William Fulton exec of Jane Fulton/Richard F. Alexander exec of Tamison Alexander /Margaret Boulden and William Taylor adm of William Boulden/James Magraw exec of Martha Moore/Timothy Kirk adm of Elisha Kirk/Timothy Kirk adm of William Mullen/Mary Gorrell adm of James Gorrell/Joshua Craig adm of Alexander Craig /William Ricketts nr Elkton, offers reward for apprentice to millering business named George Davis, about 18

38. EPM Aug 2 1823/New Store (dry goods) at stand formerly occ by Welsh & Harding - Rochester & Howard/For sale - Worsell Manor in Sassafras Neck and Bottom Meadow - George Ford of Cecilton agent for William D. Mercer/James Mathews - weaving, dying, and fulling nr Elk Landing, Cecil Co/Isaac W. Smith should contact Editor of the Virginia Times, Richmond, to hear of something to his advantage

39. EPM Aug 9 1823/It appears that the unfortunate Marshal Ney, who was shot in Paris on the restoration of the Bourbons, was born nr Elkton, Md, and that his proper name was Michael Rudolph. He rec'd first rudiments of his education in Capt. Lee's dragoons of the Maryland Line during the revolution. After his discharge he removed to Carolina where he married, but his matrimonial connexions rendered him unhappy, on which he left his family, took a vessel to the West Indies. There was no trace of him until the French government, after the execution of Ney, took possession of his papers /Democratic Meeting of Cecil Co - Gen. Hezekiah Foard, chairman; Henry Hollingsworth, sec'y/Jefferson Herdman, M.D. has commenced his practice in Kent Co/Thomas Vail exec John Lunn of St. George's Hundred, Del/George Mahan of Elkton offers reward for apprentice to coachmaking, William Merkle or Merkel, about 19, 5 ft 6-7 inch and well made; he was raised in the family of Dr. Ruan who now res in Phila/Sheriff's sale of dwelling house and tract adj lands of heirs of John Comegys and lands of William F. Abbott: prop of Benjamin Knock/Sheriff's sale of 8 a. of land of Josiah Alexander now occ by Richard F. Alexander to satisfy debt due Benjamin W. Harris adm of Benoni Harris/Sheriff's sale of 3 negro boys, prop of Carvell Hall/Sheriff's sale of tract of Jacob Johnston to satisfy debt due John Kean/Sheriff's sale of tract of David Reynolds nr Rising Sun to satisfy debt due Carvil Cooley/Sheriff's sale of prop of Samuel and Robert Kerr: two islands in Susquehanna River and house purch from John Patterson and a house where David White res

40. EPM Aug 9 1823/Sheriff's sale of 3 negroes, prop of Stephen Hyland to satisfy debt due Henry Stump/Sheriff's sale of tract of Thomas Biddle to satisfy debt due Benjamin Boulden/Sheriff's sale of tract of 301 a. of John

Hyland of Jacob to satisfy debt due William Craig and Elkton Bank/Sheriff's sale of tract of Wells and Mahan to satisfy debt due Adam Whan, use of Frisby Henderson/Sheriff's sale of tract of John Henderson to satisfy debt due James Morgan Jr/Sheriff's sale of tract of Edward Oldham Jr to satisfy debt due Roman Catholic Corporation of Md/Sheriff's sale of 3 tracts nr Elkton called New Hall, Concord and Little Anglesea, about 400 a., prop of William Kilgore to satisfy debts due James Delecourse and Delecourse & Gault/Sheriff's sale of tract, prop of Samuel Kerr to satisfy due Samuel Roland/Sheriff's sale of tract of Thomas Stephens to satisfy debt due Joseph Cosden/Sheriff's sale of tract of William Davis to satisfy debt due Andrew Harman/Sheriff's sale of tract of Lambert Beard and Andrew C. Smith to satisfy debt due William C. Hull, use of Frisby Henderson/Sheriff's sale of tract of Alexander Wilson to satisfy debt due William Craig/Sherif's sale of horses, cattle and farming utensils of William Kilgore to satisfy debt due Adam Whan, use of Sewall & Rickets/Sheriff's sale of horses, cattle, farming utensils and household and kitchen furniture of Peter Boushell to satisfy debts due Daniel Crouch /Sheriff's sale of horses, cattle, farming utensils, and household and kitchen furniture of James Scott to satisfy debts due Adam Whan, use of Sewall & Rickets/Sheriff's sale of tract called The Court House Point, 200 a. of Charles Oldham, to satisfy debts due George Peacock

41. Aug 16 1823/Died at Christiana Del Sun last, Mrs. Tabitha Nivin wife of David Nivin/For rent - Brick Store house next door to Isaac Wilson's tavern - John Aldridge/Farm for sale, about 1 1/2 mile from Elkton - Zeb Rudulph, Phila/Sheriff's sale in Octorara Hundred of John Swaggert/Sheriff's sale of lot of Thomas D. Clayton to satisfy debt due John Champan/Sheriff's sale of tract of Richard Harris of Elisha/Sheriff's sale of 400 a. of William Kilgore /Sheriff's sale of tract of Richard Simpers/Sheriff's sale of tract of William Simpers/Sheriff's sale of 1/8 of 300 a. in Elk Neck where John Manly formerly res, prop of Ann and Margaret Sevin/Sheriff's sale of tract in Bohemia Manor where Gen. Hezekiah Foard now res, prop of George W. Oldham /Sheriff's sale of farm adj lands of John Ward, Hyland Price and others, prop of Thomas Stephens

42. EPM Aug 23 1823/For sale - Brick ware house in Elkton occ by Rev John Sharpley - Joseph G. Partridge, Balt/William C. Mount, village of Newlondon Cross Roads, Chester Co, Pa, advertises stray cow/Sale of farm in Kent Co in accord with will of Mrs. Mary Scott - William Boyer, present tenant will shew prop; apply to Dr. Edward Scott, Georgetown Cross Roads or subscribers, Thomas W. Veazey, John Groome, exec of Mary Scott; also farm of Miss Sarah Black of Wilmington Del, adj above farm/William Miller exec of Dr. Abraham Tillotson/Samuel Taylor adm of John Taylor/John Conrad adm of Jacob Conrad /Jacob Biddle adm of Elizabeth Biddle/Thomas Orr adm of William Orr

43. EPM Aug 30 1823/Sale of horses, cattle, sheep and swine - Stephen Beans, Brick Hill, Cecil Co/Georgeton School is open - Robert Elliott/Washington Hotel, Elkton - Rowland Ellis/Union tavern - Joseph P. Ryland/chancery sale of a lot on Harrison St and a farm in Cecil Co occ by Nicholas Massey - J. Glenn, trustee/Samuel Dawson expelled from Fidelity Lodge No. 162 for gross unmasonic conduct/Edward Oldham adm of Patrick Barnes/Catharine Price adm of John Boyer Price/Ambrose Price adm of Susan Hays/John Wroth adm of Benjamin Knock/Samuel Karr adm of George H. Karr/Thomas Simpers adm of Jacob Simpers

44. EPM Sep 23 1823/Recommended for Gen. Assembly by Democratic Republicans of Cecil Co: 1st Dist - Dr. Guy Bryan; 2nd Dist - Frisby Henderson; 3d Dist -

Daniel Sheridine; 4th Dist - James Gerry/Kent Co Democratic Republican Ticket:
Dist 1 - James Hodges; Dist 2 - William Coburn; Dist 3 - Joseph Irland Jr;
Dist 4 - Rasin Gale/G. B. Cosden, Cecil Co, candidate for legislature/For sale
at Rock Run adj Port Deposit: 14 a. where Samuel Kerr res: fishery nr Mrs.
M'Clarrys - Samuel Kerr, Robert Kerr/Land and mills for sale; mill long know
as Porter's mill - John Harlan, M. H. Harlan

45. EPM Sep 30 1823/Married Tues by Rev Magraw, Samuel Gillespie to Miss
Hetty M'Clellan, both of Octoraro Hundred, Cecil Co/Died Tues morn last in
13th yr, Washington Wilson, eld son of Samuel Wilson of this town/Died at his
res, Brick Meeting House, Cecil Co, Wed last, Israel White, Postmaster at that
place/Died yesterday morning nr Wilmington Del, Thomas Tyson son of Mathias
Tyson of this co, member of Baptist Society/Jeremiah Cosden, about to remove
to Balt, offers to rent his house in Elkton/Candle manufactory - Virtue &
Hogg, Elkton

46. EPM Nov 8 1823/Jefferson Glenn, Atty at law, Elkton/James Salisbury
candidate for sheriff, Kent Co, Md/Sale of tract adj lands of John Conrad,
Elizabeth Walker, Mrs. Grubb, about 120 a.; also tract adj land of William
Preston and Joshua Lowe; James C. M'Dowell res on former prop - Andrew R.
Porter/Sheriff's sale of tract of Thomas Rutter where he res, to satisfy debt
due Henry Hollingsworth/John M'Ilvain, Chester Pa, offers reward for 2 mares
which strayed from pasture of Henry Hollingsworth/Dry goods - William Wingate,
North East/Reuben H. Primrose, Appoquinimink Hundred, New Castle, Del, offers
reward for stolen horse/Died Phila Wed last F. George Schaeffer, late editor
of Federal Republican of Balt, in his 30th yr/Anne Mackey exec of Catherine
Mackey/Josiah Woodrow adm of Richard Hanna/John Rawling adm of Joseph
Foxlow/William Kirk exec of Jesse Brown/Thomas Reed adm of Elry
Richardson/Mary Spring, James Sewall exec of James Springer/Ann Pugh, John
Bryan, adm of Humphrey Pugh/The Ferry House for rent at Chesapeake opp Havre
de Grace together with the right of a Team Boat; arrangement can be made with
Major Wigton, the tenant - Joshua Richardson/Levi Boulden, living in village
of Glasgow, New Castle Co, Del, offers reward for black mare/Court case - Jane
Kidd vs Robert Love; creditors of Robert Love are requested to exhibit claims

47. EPM Nov 15 1823/Samuel Kerr of Port Deposit, candidate for Gen Assembly,
to fill vacancy occasioned by death of Daniel Sheridine/Meeting to repair
Episc Church of Bohemia Manor

48. EPM Nov 22 1823/Died at Port Deposit on evening of 13 inst, Thomas Burts,
native of Ireland and for last 7 yrs of that village, leaving widow and 3
small children/Herrings, shad and hay - Purnell & Bennett, Elkton/Fall
fashions - John F. A. Biddle, tayloring business, next door to Mr. Sharpley's
store/William Webb forwarns persons from taking an assignment given by him to
Stephen Beans for $1000 (alleged non-performance of contract)/William George
on east branch of North East Creek advises of a strayed brown mare/Margaret
James, Pencader Hundred, New Castle, Del, offers reward for colt/Sheriff's
sale at house of John C. Price in Cecilton: right of John Coppin to farm in
Sassafras Neck adj lands of Thomas Stephens, Hyland Price

49. EPM Nov 29 1823/Died at his res in Sassafras Neck, after a short illness
on 24 Sep last, William F. Abbott, aged 72 yrs, leaving a widow and many
relations and friends/Public meeting of Republicans of 3d dist at Mrs.
Simpson's tavern, Col. William C. Miller, chairman, William Niblock, sec'y.

Thomas L. Savin nominated as candidate to fill vacancy occasioned by death of Daniel Sheredine/For rent - tenant house, oil mil, bark mill and saw mill nr Octoraro Bridge - James Andrews/Meliscent Abbott adm of William F. Abbott /Samuel Wilson advertises a stray horse

50. EPM Dec 13 1823/Distillery for sale - 2 stills, 1 of capacity of 144 and the other of 66 gallons and 100 hogsheads - John M'Cord, Elkton/Died at his res nr Cecilton, Mon 3d inst after a protracted indisposition, Peregrine Standley age 45/Died nr Cecilton after a short illness, Thurs 4 inst, Benjamin Price, age 23/Died at his res nr Cecilton same day, Henry Patterson, age 42, after a severe illness/Elkton Debating Society - Henry Hollingsworth, Jefferson Glenn, Joseph Gilpin, Committee/Race between horses of Charles Coleman (Bolivar) and Mr. Lyon (Roderick Dhue) for $400/For rent: 3 fisheries at Turkey Point and several negro women for hire - Samuel Thomas, Turkey Point/Louis Miller, Litle Elk, advertises about stray cattle/William Conard, Wilistown, Chester Co, Pa, offers reward for stolen horse

51. EPM Dec 13 1823/Sheriff's sale of tract of John Rogers divised to him by his father, Thomas Rogers, to satisfy debt due Henry Hollingsworth/Thomas S. Thomas, North East, offers reward for detection of person who stole a number of articles from his store/Farm for sale of late James Jones in Kent Co, Md, adj lands of Major Edward Wright, Mrs. Worrell, and Isaac Freeman/Pearce's tavern for rent, nr Back Creek, now in the possession of Thomas Biddle, together with farm (248 a.); apply to Benjamin Pearce or Collins Tatman nr Elkton or Elizabeth Pearce res at Samuel Kerr's in Kent Co, Md/C. Meginniss advertises that his wife Mary has left his bed & board; he will not pay any of her debts/For rent - Tavern stand, Ferry, and Team Boat, occ by James Knight; apply to A. J. Thomas, William Coale and John Dunn of Havre-de-Grace - George Bartol/Michael Montgomery adm of Thomas Montgomery/Catharine M'Ginnis, Phila, in care of Mathias Coats, in search of Hugh M'Ginnis who left Ireland (Milltown, six miles from city of Derry, count Derry; he sent for his dau whom he left an infant about 6 yrs ago; she left her country and relatives and came from Ireland with an uncle who in 7 weeks after arrival left her without money or friends

52. EPM Dec 27 1823/Died Fri 17 inst, Mrs. Mary Little, late consort of Christopher Little, in her 44th yr/Zeb Rudulph, Elkton, advertises that he has deposited the Universalist Church fund to accumulate interest at 4% until sufficient funds are available to build the Universalist Church/Winter goods and axes manufactured by Kidd, Thompson, Kinsey, Pugh, and M'Conchey - L. H. Evans/Sale of right of Matthew M'Laughlin to tracts: Kinsley Reads' Addition, conveyed by William Read which was assigned in the partition of real est of his father, Andrew Read; also share of William Read to prop of late John Read of Phila - Jefferson Glenn, trustee/George Davidson, Cecil Co, to petition for relief under insolvency laws/Married Tues evening last at Perry Point by Rev Duke, Levi H. Evans of Elkton, to Miss Rachel, youngest dau of John Stump/Died Sun last nr Rock Meeting, Cecil Co, Miss Ellen Perrey, aged about 22 yrs/Died 7th day of 29 ult at his res nr Rising Sun, Skipworth Coale in 40th yr/For rent - Tavern house in the west end of Elkton occ by John and Isaac Wilson - Henry Bennett, Elkton

53. EPM Dec 27 1823/Letters remaining at P.O. Elkton: Susan Anderson; John Ash; Henrietta Brisco; Edmond Brown; John Beedle; John Bryne; John Bryan; James Y. Bryan; Levi Boulden; John Brown; Oliver Blood; Jonathan Beans; James

Backum; Amelia S. Coale; Maria Coale; Ann Coale; Rebecca Chambers; Nicholas Chambers; Helen Crompton; Mr. Chamberlain; Samuel Cram; Sarah Clerke; James Davis; William Duke; John Dean; Catherine Egnor; Dennis O. Ferry; Isaac Gibbs; William Garnor; Moses Gillingham; Andrew Houck; Manuel Hall; John Henderson; William H. Hamer; John Huff; Robert Jones; James Johnson; William Kilgore; Joseph Lort; Francesina Miles; Amos Moore; Augustus Miller; William Maxwell; Jon Mathews; Reece Mahan; John Moore; James H. Morrow; George M'Donald; John M'Donald; John M'Kaige; Samuel M'Creery; Benjamin M'Kinsey; James M'Cabe; Maria Oldham; Charles Oldham; William Pennington; Catharine Price; Nancy Phillips; William Rochester; Mintus Richardson; Thomas Reed; John Robert; William Robison; Samuel C. Sample; Robert Sergeant; Mary Simpson; Henry Simpson; Jacob Stevens; Isaac Seavill; Ann Thomas; William Tyson; Abraham Tillotson; Martha Tumblin; John T. Wirt; William Warnick; Elizabeth Wallace; Jonathan Weaver; Worshipful Master of Union Lodge; Diana York - Adam Whan, P.M.

54. EPM 27 1823/Sale of real est of James Ewing by order of Orphans Court, Lancaster Co, Pa, of plantation in township of Little Britain adj lands of Robert Maxwell, William Hutton, Levin Brown, Alexander Grubb, William M'Cullough/Sale by order of Orphans Court, New Castle Co, Del, of plantation and land adj Hugh James' saw mill, being real est of Capt James Miles decd; apply to Jacob Faris and James Stewart Jr admrs - Matthew Kean, clk/John M'Cord, Elkton, to rent his tavern, Sign of the Wagon, Lancater Co, Bart Township; apply to James Andrews nr premises/George Davidson, Cecil Co, to petition for relief under state insolvency laws

55. EPM Jan 10 1824/Boot & shoe making, Chestertown, Owen C. Jones, Isaiah Coleman/Chancery Court Case -James Allen vs William Bordley and Juliana C. Bordley - William H. Barroll, trustee

56. EPM Feb 28 1824/Married Thurs 19 inst by Rev Dare, Joel Sutton of Cecil Co to Miss Margareta Lovett of Lancaster Co, Pa/Married Tues evening 10 inst by Rev Thomas Smith, John Burlage to Miss Ann Maria 2d dau of Robert Hall, all of Chestertown/Died in this village Sun last after a short illness of 17 hrs, Elizabeth A. Purnell dau of Greenbury Purnell, in 3d yr of her age/Sale of pers est of Thomas Vail, St. George's Hundred, New Castle Co, Del, nr Buck Tavern - Archibald Gordon, Andrew M'Intire/Mount Ararat for sale, 387 a., about 1 miles below Fort Deposit; apply to Ann E. Thomas on adj prop/Tanyard for rent - Henry Hollingsworth, Elkton, former occupant

57. EPM Mar 13 1824/Married Thurs 4 inst by Rev Chambers, Outen Jester to Miss Sarah Hudson, both of Bohemia Manor/Died in this village, Matthew Cantwell/Died Sat morning 21 ult, after a few hrs illness at his res on Bohemia Manor, William Orr, in 34th yr; native of Ireland; came to this country when young and has been employed for 7-8 yrs past as a school teacher; left a wife and 2 small children/A fox to be let go from the house of Robert C. Lusby - free for any hound dog or slut - Mr. Dawson's section agnst the county!/Sheriff's sale of title and interest of Richard Simpers jr to tract devised to him by Thomas Simpers sen, Cecil Co, decd, to satisfy debt due Henry D. Miller/Sheriff's sale of farm in Sassafras Neck whereon Lambert Beard res, to satisfy debt due Oliver Caulk and others/Sheriff's sale of title of Benjamin Knock, decd, to a house on road from Cecilton to Lower parts of Sassafras Neck to satisfy debt due Delacour and Gault/Henry Tilghman, QA Co and William H. Barrell, Chestertown, offer their services in the Practice of

Law/James Johnston has taken Tavern House in Port Deposit, lately occ by Brice Curran; he has removed his lumber yard from nr Mr. Smith's to opp his own house/Elizabeth Nowland, nr the Head of Sassafras, Kent Co, Md, offers reward for stolen horse.

58. EPM Mar 13 1824/Thomas Ramsay offers for sale 160 a. in New London township, Chester Co, adj lands of George Duffield, the heirs of Mary Scott and others; apply to Thomas Scott res adj or Thomas Ramsay in East Nottingham, Cecil Co/Moses Scott, Sen., nr the Elk Forge, offers reward for stolen horse, taken from the store of William Cowan in Cowantown; a William Arnat is suspected/5 shares of stock in Elkton Bank of Md for sale - Jno. W. Comegys, nr Cecilton/Plantation for sale by decree of Orphans Court of New Castle Co Del at house of John Herdman, Innkeeper, village of New Ark, Del, being real est of Joseph Waggoner, bounded by lands of Thomas Bradley, heirs of Andrew Fisher decd, and lands of Zackeus Jones: 40 a. and house - Jacob Shermizer adm of decd

59. EPM Apr 17 1824/Letters remaining at P.O. Elkton: Mary E. Alexander; Mary Alexander; Levi Alexander; John Ash; Letticia Alexander; Alexander Alexander; Samuel R. Briscoe; John Biddle; Parker Bernard; John Beedle; William Biddle; Spencer Biddle; John L. Bowman; John Bryant; Mathew Boreland; John Berry; Rebecca Crawford; John A.Cruthers; Richard Corbley; William H. Clifton; Walter Caruthers; Josiah Chick; William Colmary; Jeremiah Cosden; George Davidson; Thomas S. Dawson; Elizabeth Elias; William Fulton Jackson C. Foster; Samuel H. Freeman; Capt. Fairbanks; Eliza Grindage; John R. Giles; Ann M. Giles; Archibald Gordon; William Gerry; Edward Greeves; Sarah Gale; John Weston Holt; Samuel Hollingsworth Jr; Robert Hodgson; Samuel Hughs; Peter Howard; Alexander; Hinds; John Harris; Abraham Hawkins; Joseph Hanson;' Henderson & Bryan, Gerry & Kerr; Benedict Jones; Eliza Jobs; George Karsner; Charles Kaas; Samuel Love; John M'Clinton; Isiah M'Cluer; William M'Cummings; Benjamin F. Mackall; Thomas Polhamus; Joseph Phillips; Caroline Purnell; William Pennington; Catherine Price; William Relea; James Ramsey; Tobias Rudulph; Sarah P. Sullivan; Mary Saulsbury; Benjamin Sluyter; William Smith; Edmun Taylor; Abraham Tillotson; William Thomas; James Thomas; Rachel Veazey; James Waites; David Walker; John Walker; Nathaniel Wiley; Mary Work; William Ward; John Williamson; Worshipful Master Union Lodge No. 482 - Adam Whann, P.M.

60. EPM Apr 17 1824/Mary Redgraves adm of William M. Redgraves, Kent Co /Ploughs - William Kinkead, Elkton/For sale farm and mill seat, 130 a. in Octorara Hundred, Cecil Co, adj lands of Francis Smith, Andrew Dunbar and others - John Conrad, agent for heirs of J. Conrad, decd/Lewis Pugh and Co have established themselves in the Smithing business in East Nottingham township, Chester Co, Pa, on road from Oxford to Elkton. They will also make or repair following named screws: hoisting or mill screws, timber wheel screws, smith's vice screws, lighter screws for merchant, grist or paper mills; also new flight bars and plates for paper mill engine rolls, and dress old plates when worn dull/Married Wed evening last by Rev A. K. Russsel, Joseph Hossinger to Miss Charlotte Kerr, both of New Castle Co, Del/Shoe store No. 5 Rickett's Row - William H. Hamer, Agent, Elkton/Morning and evening - Union Line steam boats to and from Phila - A. F. Henderson, agent, Frenchtown/Lewis Chamberlin clock and watch maker, Elkton/Abraham Bennett has removed to Back Creek and taken Back Creek Tavern, formerly occ by S. Freeman

61. EPM Apr 17 1824/Teacher wanted - apply to Hyland Pennington or George Beasten, Cecilton/Spring goods - B. W. Harris, who just removed to Back Creek/Young Ladies boarding school, Newark, Del - W. Sherer /Spring Goods - Levi H. Evans, Elkton/William W. Ramsay, Carpenter's Point Fisheries, offers shad and herring for sale/Ely Balderson, Conowingo, offers reward for 2 ploughs taken by mistake or stolen; deliver to Mr. Weems at Fort Deposit or Isaiah Cooper at Conowingo. One is a three horse plough horse plough; it has a plate of iron underneath the beam, nearly or quite the whole length from the coulter to the end and the lower round at the upper end of the handle or stilt is half worn. The other is a two horse plough painted red, made by T. Ford of Baltimore; this plough has never been used although the mould board has been rubbed nearly bright/Benjamin C. Kirk forwarns persons from taking assignment on a note drawn by him for $25, payable to John Shephard of Cecil Co

62. EPM Apr 17 1824/Letters remaining at P.O. Chestertown: Unit Angier; Mrs. Margaret Briscoe; Benedict S. Brevitt; Joseph Brice; Lambert S. Beck; Mrs. Millisent Beck; James Browne; Samuel Covington; Isaiah Coleman; George Corks; Bishop S. Crossman; Joseph Cox; Jonas Crew; Mrs. Ann W. Chew; Jonathan Crew; James Diott; Mrs. Temperance Everitt; William Elett; Mrs. Margaretta Eades; Lawrence Everiott; William Foreman; John G. Graves; John Griffith; Isaac P. Groome; Thomas B. Hynson; Mrs. Sarah Jones; Miss Eliza Jones; Dr. Thomas C. Kennard; Miss Eliza L. Medford; John C. Murphy; Albert Miller; John Moore; Miss Maria Miller; Joseph Parsons; Charles Robbin; Thomas Sutton; Charles Stoney; Reuben Scoley; Miss Rebecca Thomas; Samuel Thomas; Miss Mary A. Thompson; Lieut Thomas B. Tilden; William Thomas; Joseph Usilton; Miss Antonietta Wickes; Mrs. Averilla Williams; James Wallace; Mrs. Susan E. Waltham; Mrs. Ann Wickes - Joseph Redue, P.M.

63. EPM May 1 1824/Wilmington & Elkton Mail coach will leave George Peacock's Inn, Elkton, every morning, Sunday excepted, at 6 and arrive at Eli Lamborn's Inn, Wilmington, at 10: a.m. - On the return trip, leaving Wilmington at 1 and arriving at Elkton at 5: p.m. - Fare $1.50 - These times are calculated to accommodate persons travelling between Wilmington and Baltimore via Frenchtown Steam Boat/Died Sat 24 ult after a lingering and painful illness, Miss Rachel Howard aged 30, dau of late William Howard of Prospect Hill of this co, member of Meth Church/Dry Goods - Samuel R. Hogg, 2 doors east of Mr. Peacock's Inn/G. B. Cosden, Atty at Law, Elkton, has removed to a lot nr ofice formerly occ by Davidson David and nr former res of Thomas Giles decd, avail there or at Mr. Beasten's/Boot & shoe manufactory - James Chamberlin & Son, opp Mr. Peacock's Inn/Election of town Commissioners (seven) to be held - Evan D. yates, clk/Sale of pt of tract, Yorkshire with stone dwelling house presently occ by George Davidson, about 1 1/2 mile south of Port Deposit; also 1/3 pt of Thomas Fishery - Levin Gale, trustee/William Smith has removed from borough of Strasburg to tavern in Martick township, Lancaster Co, Pa /James Riddle reports finding stray mare/Election of directors of Elkton Bank of Md - P. Harding, cash'r/Dissolution of partnership of John Virtue and Samuel R. Hogg, Elkton/Dry goods - William Wingate, North East/Commissioners of Tax for Cecil Co to hear appeals - John Kean, clk

64. EPM May 8 1824/Died at his res Middletown Del Thurs 20 ult, Richard Gerritson in his 60th yr/Died Sat last, Anthony Higgins, of the vincinity of St. Georges Del/Sale of household and kitchen furniture - Mary Howard, Prospect Hill/Land for sale, 94 a. being 1/2 of Plumb Point Farm, late the prop of Nicholas Wingate in Elk Neck; apply to Henry Wingate or George

Ricketts/Adam Short offers reward for 4 five-dollar notes, 3 of which are on the Elkton Bank of Md and the other on the Canandaigua Bank, N.Y.

65. EPM May 15 1824/Senior officers of the District Companies attached to the 49th Regt of Maryland Militia are requested to enrol immediately all persons within their districts, subject to militia duty ... assemble the Companies ... and nominate suitable persons to fill vacancies in their respective companies, and report the same to the Colonel, on or before 1st of July next. By order, Robert C. Lusby, Adj't/Tailoring business in the house lately occ by Michael Martin, next door to the jail - Adam Purves/Robert Knight, Tailor, has taken the shop recently occ by J. F. A. Biddle opp Mr. Peacock's Tavern, Elkton (keeping an experienced cutter employed)/Daniel Kendrick insolvent debtor discharged from imprisonment/For sale at the house of Abijah Fenn at Conowingo, a tract called Porter's and Grubb's Folly, on Susquehanna at the head of the Maryland Canal and binding on Arkhaven; contains a bed of coal. Apply to James C. M'Dowell agent for Richard Caton or Francis Forster, Balt/Chancery sale of a farm in Cecil Co, nr the Rock Meeting house, occ by Mary Wallaston, about 21 a., at Blue Ball tavern; Alexander Alexander will shew or call on David Mackey, trustee/Samuel Kerr exec of Rev. Thomas Sewell

66. EPM May 22 1824/Alexander Boulden appointed post master at Churchtown (Bohemia Manor)/Dwelling house of George Turner, at Broad Creek, consumed by fire Fri 14 inst; caused, it is said, by the chimney taking fire/Married by Rev Duke, William Jones to Miss Susan M'Kinsey, all of this village/Rev James Magraw will preach to the Court House tomorrow evening/Dr. Parker has removed to the New Building opp Mr. Lusby's tavern, Elkton/Elkton Troop of Cavalry to meet at Mr. Z. Beasten's Inn, Elkton, to re-organize the troop and elect a Captain and other officers. As a number of the old officers and men are now over age, it is hoped that others will come forward and enrol themselves. - William Roberts, Captain/Volunteers are requested to attend meeting at Cross Keys Tavern, Brick Meeting House, to consider forming a Volunteer Company/Small net found on shore of subscriber - J. B. Sims, Poplar Neck, Cecil Co/Conowingo Fair

67. EPM May 29 1824/Died 15 inst, Major John J. Coxe of Sassafras Neck, in this co, decided Republican/Meeting of Levy Court of Cecil Co - James Sewall, clk/Meeting of Commissioners of Tax for Cecil Co - John Kean, clk/The Elkton Light Infantry Company will parade on the Academy Lot Sat 5 June at 4 o'clock, p.m. - Henry Stump, Capt/Hats & shoes - William H. Hamer, agent/Summer goods & nails - L. H. Evans/For sale - mill seat and 150 a. of land adj. This seat has a fall of 70 ft, a race that never fails; stone on the premises to build a town, within 3 miles of North East Church, from which run regular packets to Balt - apply to Joseph G. Partridge, Balt, or Joseph Harlon nr the premises or Henry Hollingsworth in Elkton; also for sale: prop in Elkton occ by Rev Jno. Sharpley as a dry goods and grocery store

68. EPM (Elkton Press & Cecil advertiser) Nov 1 1828/Joseph Mendenhall seeks families with children to work in the Endeavour cotton Factory, nr Stanton, in Delaware/William Garrett continues to have wool carded into rolls, or manufactured into cloths, cassimeres or blankets at his Mills, 7 miles above Elkton. Wool will be rec'd at the stores of Messrs Wingate & Manly, Elkton - Benjamin W. Harris, Back Creek - Alfred Nowland, Cecilton/Elisha Kirk and John Marshall exec of Dr. James Beard/John M. Johnston adm of Rachel

Ricketts/Dr. J. H. Scott, offers his professional services to inhabitants of Charlestown/Canal Packet Boat, Lady Clinton, running to and from Delaware City, St. Georges, Summit Bridge on the Chesapeake and Delaware Canal - H. Hugg, Phila, T. Mulford, St. Georges/Joseph B. Sims nr Cantwell's Bridge, New Castle Co, Del, offers reward for negro, George Anderson, about 21-22, rather stout built; a few days before he absconded he attempted to commit a rape upon a young female of his own color, the punishment for which, has caused his running off/Steam Boat Patuxent to land and take off at Georgetown and Frederick on the Sassafras

69. EPM Nov 1 1828/Joseph Townsend, Balt City, and Jeremiah Brown and Slater Brown of Little Britain, Lancaster Co, exec of Joseph England, Cecil Co, decd /Henry Jamar seeks apprentice to blacksmithing business/Rev Williamson will preach in the Court House/Long article on Ohio, "one of the most flourishing states in the Union," 4th in population. Meeting of the Friends of the Administration of the General Government at the house of S. H. Freeman, Back Creek/To elect Elector for President and Vice-President of U. S. - Thomas Miller, Jr., Sheriff/Nicholas Vandegrift, having conveyed to a company of gentlemen the exclusive sporting privilege of Welch Piont and adj shores, does forwarn all persons from trespassing on said premises/Elkton Races - R. C. Lusby - 1st day, 2 miles and repeat for purse of $100; 2nd day 3 miles and repeat for purse of $200; 3rd day 1 mile, 3 best of 5 for purse of $50

70. EPM Nov 8 1828/Centreville Times reports that Capt Taylor of Steam Boat Maryland, while lying at Easton Point on Tues last, had his desk broken open and about $9000 stolen...principal part belonged to a person in Baltimore, left with capt T. to deposit in Annnapolis Bank/Mrs. Mary Corse of Kent Co was thrown from her carriage, a few days since, and her breast so mangled by a corner of the vehicle, that she died in abaout half an hour... About 2 yrs since, her brother was thrown from a gig and killed and about 18 months since, her husband also was killed by a log rolling from a wagon on him, and crushing him to death - Centreville Times

71. EPM Nov 18 1828/Married at Robert C. Lusby's in Elkton Tues last 11 inst, by Rev Andrew Barratt, John R. Price to Miss Rachel Wolmsley/Married at same place, on same day, Harrison S. Bullen to Mary Price, all of this co /Married Tues 11 inst by Rev William Ryder, Isaac Hines, of Kent Co, Md, to Miss Ann Knock, of QA Co/Sheriff's sale at the house of Robert Penington: 2 horses, 2 milch cows, 1 waggon and right to land where he res, about 30 a., adj lands of Mrs. Ann B. Ferot and Benjamin B. W. Chambers, at suits of Benjamin B. W. Chambers, surviving exec of Nicholas Chambers/Joshua Hyland forwarns persons from trespassing on Plumb Point/Port Deposit - Following have attended lectures on English Grammar by Dr. Cleaveland and recommend him to the public: John Creswell, William T. Prigg, Edward Emmons, J. W. Abrahams, John Sinnott, W. B. Stevens/Farm & fishery for rent on Bohemia, formerly belonging to late William Craig Jr - Mary Craig/Sale of farm and horses, cattle, hogs, oxen, carts and furniture - William Lee, Grove Point, Cecil Co/Swaims Panacea at my Medicine and Drug Store - Caleb Parker, Elkton

72. EPM Nov 22 1828/Results of Elkton Races on Wed 12 inst; weather was unfavorably wet/Hon. David J. Campbell of Kent Co died; represented his co in Gen Assembley during session of 1826 and subsequently re-elected/Singing school - John Whann/For rent - merchant mill and dwelling house, now in the

-19-

tenure of James G. Moore and farm nr Frey's Forge in the tenure of Richard Keetly; also farm in Elk Neck in the possession of Augustus Stoops and house in Elkton which formerly belonged to Jeremiah Cosden; house opp Edward Wilson; 2 small shops occ by Jacob Anderson; frame house occ by John Lindsey; frame house occ by Edward Short; house occ by H. L. Biddle - apply at Elkton Bank of Maryland, W. Wingate, cashier

73. EPM Dec 6 1828/Meeting of Commissioners of Cecil Co - William Hewitt, clk/blacksmith wanted - John Rawlins or Joseph Bryan, Bohemia Manor/For rent - dwelling house and storehouse; also dwelling and cartwright shop - Samuel Freeman, Back Creek Mills/O. Horsey, Cliffs, Cecil Co, seeks to hire negro men

74. EPM Dec 13 1828/Married Thurs 27 ult in Phila by Rev Thomas Dunn, Solomon Sharpe, M. D. of Christiana, Del, to Miss Catherine Marion Harris, of Cecil Co/Married Thurs last by John Crosgrove, Justice of the Peace for Chester Co, John Wilson to Jane Talley, both of New Castle Co/Married Sun last at Cantwell's Bridge, New Castle Co, Del, by Rev William Ryder, Samuel Cooper to Miss Sarah Harris/New goods at the Cheap Store - Thomas Howard Jr/To rent Tavern House and Ferry at Chesapeake opp Havre de Grace, now occ by Coale and Penington - J. Richardson/Thomas Sturgeon adm of James Sturgeon

75. EPM Dec 20 1828/Rev Dr. Clowes, Ecclesiastical Superintendent of P.E. Churches in Cecil, Kent, QA, to preach at several places/Married Thurs evening last by Rev Woolford, Abel C. Davis of this place to Rachael Wallace of Pearch Creek/Died in Sansbury Pa, 4 ult, Jacob Baker, aged 102, born in Germany Aug 1726 and emigrated to America in 1740; served in the Revolutionary War/Sale of fishing utensils - Elias Glenn

76. EPM Dec 27 1828/Accidental death of son of Phillip Rasin of Kent Co Md (by hanging)/Married at Wilmington Del Mon last, by Rev Higgins, Ellis Jones to Miss Mary W. Pryce, both of this place

77. EPM Jan 10 1829/James W. Williams, Priestford, Harf Co, candidate for congress/Died nr New Castle Del Sat 27 ult, Samuel Barr in 92nd yr, member of Presbyterian Church about 60 yrs and elder more then 40 yrs, leaving great grandchildren/WilliamD. Mercer candidate for Gen Assembly from 1st Elect Dist, Cecil Co/Lewis H. Foote candidate for Gen Assembly/Edward S. Keasby, intending to remove from Elkton in the Spring, desires to settle accounts; has general assortment of hats on hand/Store for rent in Elkton formerly occ by subscriber, Alex. Scott/Meeting of Bible Society of Cecil Co - F. Henderson, Pres

78. EPM Jan 17 1829/Independent Citizen states that the store house and stock of goods of Edward J. Markland of Darlington, Harf Co, consumed by fire Wed morning, 7 inst; loss estimated at $4,000. Family escaped with difficulty/Lewis H. Foote declines candidacy/Jesse Boulden candidate for Gen Assembly/Johnson Simpers, North East, candidate for Gen Assembly/To rent farm (with fishery) on North East River belonging to William Taylor (of Phila) now in possession of Edward Pearce - John C. Groome, Elkton/Evan White, Elkton, candidate for legislature/Sale of farm late res of Major John R. Evans, decd - Mary W. Evans, exec/James Massey, nr Queens Town, adm of J. E. Denny, offers reward for negro boy, Thomas, about 18, who ran away about 2 yrs before, in the lifetime of his master, John E. Denny nr Wye Mill, QA Co. He was taken up

by Oct 1827 at Newark Del; however Tom's father, Jacob, living on a small tenement of Dr. Groome's nr Elkton, may hav seduced him away

79. EPM Jan 17 1829/Letters remaining at P.O., Elkton: Richard F. Alexander; Alex Alexander; Robert Atherton; Samuel Baker; James Boltin; Joseph Bryan; Spencer Biddle; John Bates; Mary Brisley; Edmund Brown; Henry Boram; David Ball; Ann Bennett; Thos Bayard; Augustin Biddle; Eliza Clayton; Mary Cunningham; Mary E. H. Clayland; Ann Conner; John H. Conkey; Hugh Dougherty; Abraham Davis; James R. Dawning; Francis Carothers; William Denison; Margaret Evans; S. H. Freeman; Dennis O Farry; C. F. Gangel; Joseph George; Jona Greenwood; Wm Gardener; Rich'd Green; Sabus Grifen; Mary Hassen; Auterbridge Horsey; Sarah Hutchison; Stephen Hendricks; John Jenness; Thomas Dominique; Amelia Kirk; Kolan Kawky; Elizabeth Lyerson; John M Lackey; Thomas Laire; Elijah Moore; John S. Manlove; William McCalla; Davis Mackey; John McCauley; Wm Marppongen; John L. Morgan; Maria Oldham; Thos Owens; Geo Pennington; Joseph P. Ryland; Joseph Reynolds; Wm D. Riely; Elizabeth Smith; Edward Sillitoe; John L. Stone; John Sherer; ___ Stump, Esq.; Benj. Smith; John Sherlack; Jane Sherer; Henry Staten;___ Towsend, Esq; Wm. Thomas; Ann Taylor; Levi Todd; Ann Thomas; Thomas S. Thomas; Rachel Underwood; Easter White; Mary Wagner; Wm. Warnuk; George Waller; Perry Ward; John Webberts; John Wilson - Adam Whann, P.M

80. EPM Jan 17 1829/Leters remaining P. O. Port Deposit: Mary Ann Chance; Jacob Cole; Underhill Dann; Samuel Harson; Catharine Johnson; Wm. N. Jackson; Lag Keveneugh; Rev Mr. Magraw; Wm. H. Outtin; James Snell; William Smith; John Smith; John P. Turner; George Thomas; W. Master Harmony Lodge, No. 53 - S. Nesbit, Jr. P.M

81. EPM Jan 24 1829/Hugh Wallis elected to Gen Assembly form Kent co to fill vacancy left by death of David J. Campbell/Married in Wilmington Del Tues evening 13 inst by Rev Isaac Purdee, David Cross to Miss Aceniah Sharp, both of Cecil Co/Died in Sadsbury township, Chester Co, Pa, 31 Dec last, Joseph Cloud aged 63, Magistrate of the Commonwealth, leaving widow and 5 children /Died Mon 12 inst at his res in QA Co, Capt Joshua W. Massey/For rent - house, upper wharf and store house at Elk Landing - Henry Hollingsworth /Sheriff's sale at house of William George, right of Jeremiah Short to land where he now res, about 100 a. in Elk Neck adj lands with Richard Simper, Margerey Aldridge, at suit of Samuel Miller/Patricious Finegan, from London, has commenced the tailoring business opp Mr. Peacock's Hotel

82. EPM Jan 31 1829/Married Tues 13 inst by Gardner Furness, James Gillespie to Miss Eliza M'Ellary, both of Cecil Co/Henry Andrews, nr Elkton, wishes to contract for 80,000 to 100,000 bricks/For sale - farm where I now res nr North East, pt of tract, Story's Meadows, 204 a.; also pt of tract Geferison, and pt of John & Mary's Highland - Richard Simpers/Sheriff's sale at inn of John M'Corkle - right of Patrick McGoldrick to tract on which he res, in Octorora Hundred, about 100 a., at suit of State of Maryland/Sheriff's sale of Benedict Pennington's right to land now occ by James Johnson, about 130 a. in Elk Neck, at suit of John Partridge

83. EPM Feb 7 1829/Married Tues 27 ult by Rev T. Clowes, William P. Worrell, to Miss Catharine Tilden, all of Kent Co/Married in Wilmington Mon 20 ult by E. W. Gilbert, Henry L. Peckard to Miss Mary Cann, both of Christiana Bridge /Died in this place Feb 1 in 41st yr of her age, Mrs. Rebecca Jones, consort

-21-

of George Jones and dau of Philip and Mary Rodman of Brandywine Hundred, New Castle Del. In the summer of 1809 at a Camp Meeting nr Chester Pa she was made a partaker of the Grace of God. She left a husband and 8 small children /Peter Coe has resigned his situation in the English Department of the Elkton Academy/For rent - Farm and fishery on Elk River where John Gooding res called Locust Point - Andrew M'Intire

84. EPM Feb 21 1829/The office of the Elkton Press is removed to the Brick Building opp the Court House between store of Messrs George R. Howard and Wingate & Manly/Up to 9 inches of snow!/Message from Proprietors of Elkton Press: Charles F. Cloud and John H. Conkey/Married Wed evening 11 inst by Rev Timothy O'Brien, German M'Clure to Miss Charity Quinlan all of Harf Co /Married Tues 10 inst by Rev Thomas Smith, William Edwards to Miss Mary Reed, all of Kent Co/Married Tues evening 10 inst by Rev Thompson, William Stevens, merchant of Centreville, to Miss Louisa dau of Major J. Massey of QA Co/Died in Kent Co Thurs 12 inst, Joseph Hephron/Died in the same co, same day, Colonel Thomas Wilson/For rent - house occ by subscriber nr Mr. Gale's saw mills and a fishery - Joseph Gurlie/Mill for rent known as Gilpin's Mill, 1 mile north of Elkton, on Big Elk Creek - Henry H. Gilpin/House for rent now in the tenure of Henry Hastings - Henry Jamar, George Jones/For rent - house and shop nearly opp Bank in Elkton; apply to William Mahan, res on premises or subscriber, William Robinson, nr Wilmington Del/Commissioners appointed to partition real est of William Mullen, Cecil Co, decd: John C. Cameron, Jacob Price, Tobias Biddle, Joseph Harlan, Samuel Marnes/For sale - farm, house and store adj Dr. Groome's and house and lot opp George Peacock's - Robert Johnston/English Department of Elkton Academy lately vacated is now furnished with a teacher; school is under superintendence of Mr. Jeremiah Cosden - Zeb. Rudulph, Sec'y/House on Back St for rent, occ at present by John Rarick - James Sewall

85. EPM Feb 28 1829/Thomas Williams adm of Samuel Miller/David R. Longfellow adm of Gideon Longfellow/Thomas A. Biddle adm of Andrew Biddle/Henry G. Simpers adm of Jacob Simpers/Mary W. Evans adm of John R. Evans/Henry Bennett adm of Henry Bennett/James Cameron adm of Matthew Cameron

86. EPM Mar 7 1829/Died 4 inst at his res in Elk Neck, Cecil Co, of a painful and protracted illness, Major Nicholas Hyland, leaving aged mother and wife/For sale - tract of 110 a., by virtue of will of James Springer, adj lands of Benjamin F. Mackall - Mary Springer, James Sewall, exec/House and shop for rent at present occ by John S. Taylor - Samuel Hollingsworth, Jr/For rent - dwelling house, store house, barn and stables, at intersection of road from Elkton down the Peninsula and the Chesapeake and Del Canal - George Turner, Back Creek/Horse, Marshal Ney, will stand - Samuel Hollingsworth Jr/John Stump exec of John Stump/Maria Rudulph adm of Tobias Rudulph/John Megredy adm of Thomas Hall/Henry M'Vey adm of Andrew Dunbar/Maria Jones adm of Thomas Jones/Spencer Biddle adm of Richard F. Alexander

87. EPM Mar 21 1829/Appointments: Orphan's Court: Frisby Henderson, Enoch Cloud, Thomas W. Veazy - Justices of the Peace: James Kilgour, Alexander Kinkead, John Wroth, John Jordon, George Beaston, Stephen Bayard, Samuel Guy Jr, Robert Evans of Jas, Samuel Ramsay, Hezekiah Foard, Taylor Reynolds, John M'Corkle, Enoch Cloud, William Hewitt, Benj. W. Harris, Benedict Jones, Josiah L. Foard, Elias Pennington, Cyrus Oldham, John Mackey, Charles Harris, Levi Sidwell, Zachariah B. Graham, Thomas Gale, Andrew Barrett, William Cowan,

Jacob Price, James Purnell, John Maulden, William Mackey, John S. Moffitt, Michael Trump, George W. Lightner, William S. Coale, John B. Morton, Benedict Craddock, George Gillispie, Samuel Hayes, James Rowland, Henry Chamberlain, Thomas Reynolds, Robert Hart, James Cameron, George Sanders, William A. Hall, John Rawlins, William Pierce, Spencer Biddle, William Hogg, Joseph Bryan, Richard F. Alexander, James Mitchell, John M. Flintham, Abr'm F. Pennington, Benj. T. Sluyter, James Craig, Thomas Warburton, James Broughton, John Marshall, Caleb Edmundson, Edward Emmons, John Ewing, Jacob Williams – Coroners: Peregrine L. Lynch, Charles G. Black, John Ross, James Eagan, John Watson, Thomas Moore, John Ash, John Rawlings, John F. Ryan, Hezikiah Foard Jr, George R. Howard – Fish Inspectors: for North East River, Thomas Burns; for Susquehanna River, William Orr – Lumber Inspector at Port Deposit: John McCullough – Surveyor: Henry Hollingsworth; Guager and Inspector of Spiritous Liquors at Port Deposit: Thomas Bond

88. EPM Mar 21 1829/Married Sun evening 15 inst by Rev J. Hagany, Maj. Geo Gillaspy, to Mrs. Sarah Hannah, both of the vincinity of Newport Del/Married Mon 16 inst by Rev J. Hagany, Spencer Howard, to Miss Ann Macklan, both of the vicinity of New Ark, Del/Died in this place, on Mon morning last after a short illness, Mrs. Martha Rochester in the 51st yr of her age/Died in Chestertown, Kent Co, on Tues 10 inst, Miss Sarah Ann Nichols/Died in Harf Co Sat last, Walter Bull, at an advanced age/Farm for sale at the house of George Peacock in Elkton; farm is in Sassafras Neck called Belhaven, late the prop of Thomas Stevens and formerly prop of Susanna Stevens/Tract of land for sale in vicinity of Elkton, binding on Dogwood Run – A. D. Hollingsworth, J. Hollingsworth and William Hollingsworth, exec of L. Hollingsworth/William H. Calvert has commenced hat manufacturing business at house formerly occ by Mrs. Waggoner, directly opp dwelling of Henry Hollingsworth/Sale at res of Major Nicholas Hyland decd: two large seines, about 150 fathom of New Seine of shad and hering mesh, and about 20 Fishermen's Blankets; and at the fishing shore on the east side of North East river, lately occ by Major Hyland known by the name of the Negro Swamp Fishery, the residue of the fishing materials of said Hyland, consisting of Reels, Hand-Barrows, Baskets and other articles, being the pers est of late Nicholas Hyland of Edward – Ruth Hyland and Henry Hollingsworth adm of Nicholas Hyland (of Edward) /Sheriff's sale a farm in Cecil co adj land of Alexander Scott, Jesse Simpers, prop of late Lewis Miller to satisfy debt due Elizabeth Briscoe, adm of Samuel Briscoe/Horse, Tuckahoe, will stand at the farm of Col. James Sewall, nr Elkton – Samuel R. Briscoe, Agent

89. EGM Mar 21 1829/Jacob Biddle, Elkton, offers reward for negro man, Elijah Butler, rather a light black, about 21-22, 5 ft 6-7 inch/White pine boards and plank – Ross & Wiley, Head of Maryland Canal, or Ark Haven /Sheriff's sale of right of Elizabeth H. Price to land where she res in Sassafras Neck at suit of Thomas Kennard adm of James Corse, use of Mary P. Corse adm of Unit Corse/Sheriff's sale of right of Hozea Terry to land where he res, 30 a., at suit of State of Md/Sheriff's sale of horses, cattle, sheep, hogs and farm of Peter Bouchel/Sheriff's sale of house occ as a tavern by Mouson Watkins nr Port Deposit, prop of John Creswell, at suit of Colin F. Hale/House for rent on Main St at East end of Elkton – Jacob Ash/Sherif's sale of house in Port Deposit of Samuel Gilmore at suit of John Edmondson /Sherif's sale of right of Charles Oldham to tract, Court house Point, about 400 a. at suit of Louis Price & Co, use of Israel Reynolds

90. EGM Mar 28 1829/Spring Goods - at his new stand which Robert C. Lusby occ as a tavern - Thomas Howard Jr/Dissolution of partnership of Thomas Bond and William Doughty; Thomas Bond, Port Deposit, has associated himself with William F. Savin (country store)/Proprietors of improved patent morticing machine for Cecil Co: Joel Smedley, Isaac Brown, John Fulton; Conawingo/Hugh Doughty & Son, Tailors, occ house lately occ by James Morrow/Dissolution of partnership of Lloyd M. Norris and John Raitt, Balt

91. EPM Apr 4 1829/Married Tues evening last by Rev Thomas Smith, William McDaniel to Mrs. Milcah Wilkins all of Chestertown/Married 24 ult by Rev Daniel Higbee, Gideon Waples, merchant, of Milton, Del, to Mrs. Sarah Cottingham, dau of Miers Burton, merchant, nr Millsboro, Del/Married nr Newark Del Tues evening by Rev A. K. Russel, John H. Thomas, of Cecil Co, to Mis Susan Lindsey of New Castle Co, Del/Died in Easton Sat morning, Thomas W. Loockerman, Register of the Land Office of the Eastern Shore/Died in Belle Air, Md, 24 ult, Dr. Alonzo Preston, in 33d yr/Died at the res of his uncle, R. Alison, M. D., in London-Grove, Chester Co, Pa, on 21st inst, Francis Alison Hesson, son of William Hesson of Cecil Co, in 22d yr of his age/Died 24 Dec at Nice Italy where he was res for the benefit of his health, Nathan Baynard, of Centreville, Md, in 22d yr of his age/Died 7 ult at Jericho, L. I. Jemima, consort of Elias Hicks, in 79th yr, born in same house in which she died; interred at Friends burying ground at Jericho, on 19th, at the close of a large and solemn meeting in which Elias Hicks (who was that day 81 yrs old) gave a feeling and interesting account of their union of 58 years /Spring goods - Zebulon Rudulph and William Torbert Jr, Elkton/Cabinet making - Justus Dunbar, next door to Robert Burchell's chair manufactory/For rent - dwelling house and other buildings, now occ by John McCorkle, 2 miles from Conawingo bridge - Henry McVey adm of Andrew Dunbar/Nathan Hiles nr Rising Sun, Cecil Co, seeks apprentice to tanning business/William Camp has taken Fountain Inn, Chester Town, formerly kept by Thomas Peacock and lately by Mr. C. C. Money/Horse, Algiers, will stand - R. C. Lusby/Stockholders of New Castle and Frenchtown Turnpike Company will meet - Kensey Johns Jun., Pres; James Couper, Sec'ry - New Castle, Del

92. Apr 4 1829/Letters remaining at P. O. Elkton: Capt. John Allen; Hannah Askew; Rachel Austen; Ann Boulden; John Berry; Miss Mary Ann Burk; Lambert W. Biddle; Joshua Burgain; Levy Clarkson; John Campbell; Ann Carson, care of D & A C Draper; Robert Curry; William Damsel; Richison Dunn; Miss C. Dysart; James R. Downing; Miss Araminta Downing; Jonas Elias; Margaret Egner; Miss Kitty Evans; H. Foard Jr; Dennis Fery; Samuel B. Foard; Jacob R. Garrett; W. H. Gilpin; Thomas Giles; William H. Graves; John Gooden; Alex E. Grubb; Wm Hollingsworth; Herman Husband; James Hubart; Isaac Holt; Hannah Hendricks; Henry Hastings; Robert Johnson; Francis Jarvis; Elizabeth Kerr; Wm Lee; P. L. Lynch; Revd M. Lepenette; Miss Ann Little; Thomas Miller Jr; John Marsell; John Malome; James Marley; Judges of the Orphans' Court; Margaret M'Cauley; Rev Thomas Miller; Miss Mary Pennington; Miss C. Purnell; David Porter; Jacob Pribe; Elias Pennington; James Parker & Co; John Ross; John Rawlings; John Rirack; Frisby Snow; Charles Scarborough; Henry Stewart; John Scarborough; Wm Thompson; Lavinea Thomas; Thos S. Thomas; Mathias Tyson; Sarah Vogdes; Lynix Waters; William Warnick; John Wilson; John D. Wherry; Miss Sarah Wallace; Saml Williamson; Ester White; Thos Worrell Jr; Perry Ward; Wm Whitelock; Rev Moses Williamson - Adam Whann, P.M.

93. APL Oct 1 1805/Camp meeting 10 Oct on new road from Balt to Harford, about 2 miles above Mr. Harry D. Gough's/Henry Stump, Reuben Stump and Benjamin Silver, Harf Co, to petition to clear a road from Darlington to intersect road from Belle-Air to Havre-de-Grace, nr a place called Stump's old fields/James Gallion, living on the head of Delph creek, offers reward for mulatto man, Frederic, about 6 ft, spare made, age about 23

94. BUM Jul 25 1822/Insolvent debtors of Harf Co, discharged from inprisonment: Bennet Bussey, John Rockhold, Isaac Allen, Larkin Cox/Black girl for sale - Samuel Nesbitt Jr, Port Deposit/Wanted - black boy of free parents to be bound til age - A. J. Thomas, Havre-de-Grace/Sheriff's sale postponed, of prop of Z. O. Bond at suit of Levy Court of Harf Co; also prop of Abraham Jarrett at suit of same; also prop of William S. Amos at suit of same; Samuel Ady and Thomas W. Ayres at suit of William Richardson; also sale of prop of Christian Berg and others at suit of John Archer; sale of prop of Thomas Butler at suit of Abraham Jarrett, use of Havre-de-Grace Bank and prop of John Nelson at suit of William M. Dallam; - Samuel Bradford, Sheriff /Sheriff's sale of land and tenements of John Scarburough: tract called Clark's Dunmurry and Antrim, 134 a., to satisfy a judgement due to John W. Stump and John Archer exec of John Stump - Jason Moore, late Sheriff/James White, about 2 miles from Bush, on post road, Harf Co, offers reward for apprentice lad named John Perry, about 20, 5 ft 10 inch, dark complexion, a wheelright and blacksmith/Sale of land directed by will of Benedict Edward Hall, decd: pt Sidney Park farm nr Swan Creek; Mulberry Point, about 200 a. and other land - Henry Hall, Walter T. Hall, adm/Seed Buckwheat - John Johnson and Co, Bush/

95. BUM Jul 25 1822/Letters remaining at P. O. Belle Air: R. N. Allen; James Ady; Edward Ashton; Ma... Alexander; Samuel W. Airs; Benj... Amoss; Jacob Balderston; Samuel Baxter; John Butler; Mifflin ... ; Thomas Brynam (Care of William Miller); Joseph Bell; Edward F. Bussey; Samuel Bradford; Robert Bowen; James Calden; Thomas Clark; Mr. Curry; Richard Cary; Daniel Cullom; James Cole; Sophia Calden; William Carr; Henry Dorsey; John Devoe; G. Davis; Samuel Ecoff; Shadrick R. Gilbert; Thomas Gorrell; William Gladden; A. J. Greme; Robert Gaver; Mary Harry; John T. Hughes; Abm Huff sen.; Abm Har...(care Nicholas Cooper); Rev George S. Harper; Patrick Holland; R. W. Holland(?); B. G. Jones; ...Johnson; Henry H. Johns; Morin...; Jane(?) Johnson; William H. Kennard; William Kerr; Mary Forwood; Rev John R. Keech; Jabez Kirkwood; Alexander M. Kerr; William Love; John Lee; Elizabeth Little; John M'Carnan; John M'Carey (care of John Foster); John M'...medty; Joseph Moore; W. M. Mt at Lodge 5; Thomas Norton; Thomas Poteet; John Rockhold; R... Richardson; James Rogers; Joshua Rutledge(?); Henry Ruff; Mary Rutledge; Ester Rush; ....; Henry Scarf; William Stu...; James Smith; Samuel Scarbrough; Thomas Street of Thomas; Hanna Street; ...nston D. Smith; Ulrick Tupli; Thomas Thompson; Josias Thompson; Benjamin Toland; Daniel Taylor; Joshua Wyle; Ja... Wheeler; Vintentia Waterman - John M'Kenney Jr, PM

96. BUM Jul 25 1822/Letters remaining at P.O. Havre-de-Grace: Charlotte Atkinson; John Barret; Enos Bradfield; Samuel Barsen (for Dr. Benjamin Marsh); William Brooks; Zephaniah ...; Carvel Culey; Mary C. Coal; John W. Carlile; Miss Phebe Cox; John Dun; Dr. William Dallam; Alfred P. Edwards; Sally Ford; Mrs. Ann Fowler; Luke Griffith; Learnerd Garret; Jesse Hartley; Capt Henry Hall; Edward Hall (care of J. C. C. Hall); Walter T. Hall; Clark Hyatt; Mary Hawkins; Thomas Johnson; Levi Keerens; Hannah Morgan; James Miller (A. Jarrett's fishery); Capt Murphy; George Moor; John Monamis (care of Jos.

(Jas. ?) Smith; Ellis M'Clanskey; Bernard Malone or Mr. Barton; Thomas Patterson (Rock Run); William Price (innkeeper); David Silver; Robert Suezenier; Joseph Scott; Henry C. Smith; Thomas West; Benedict F. Warter; Capt James Williams; William H. Warner - J. P. Bunting, P.M.

97. BUM Jul 25 1822/R. N. Allen will remain in Belle-Air every Tues to transact law business/Stevenson Archer will attend his ofice every Tues/Otho Scott, Atty at Law will attend every day at his office/Kimble and Duncan - saddle & harness makers, Mount Vernon, Harf Co/A tailor wanted - W. H. Cunningham, Conowingo/Dry goods & groceries - Joshua Guyton Jr, Belle Air, in the corner house that formerly belonged to John C. Brown adj Samuel Bradford /New establishment - John Bulkley & Co has taken the store lately occ by Jacob Lewis & Co in Havre-de-Grace, a few rods south of the Bank - groceries, dry goods and hard ware. Vessels suitable for the transportation of stone from Havre-de-Grace to Old Point Comfort will find constant employment/Peter Kitchen requests payment from persons indebted to him for the season of mares to horse, Paddy Whack - settle with the following named persons at the several stands: John W. Crawford, Darlington; Timothy Keen, Hall's Cross Road; Jacob Michael, Bush River Neck/Sheriff's sale at suit of Robert Careins, use of William Careins, prop of Henry Macatee; yoke of oxen, black cow, light waggon/Sheriff's sale of land whereon Richard Deaver (of James) now res, 128 a. and 1 stack of rye, 2 stacks of oats, 2 milch cows and 1 heifer, late the prop of Richard Deaver/Sheriff's sale at suit of Aquila Nelson: a negro girl named Rosetta, late the prop of Isaac Wilson and cart and oxen, late the prop of William Wilson and 1 horse late the prop of William Patterson/Sheriff's sale of right of Amos Silver and James Silver to land called Mary's Lot, 300 a., at suit of Susquehanna Bridge and Bank Co, and at the suit of Henry Woolsey; also 2 cows, prop of Gersham Silver

98. BUM Jul 25 1822/Sheriff's sale of right of Thomas Courtney to tracts, Brown's Discovery, 400 a., at suit of Daniel Pendleton and Samuel Bare, use of Samuel R. Smith/Sheriff's sale of tract called Spencer's Meadow-ground, 107 1/4 a., prop of Marshall Baldwin, at suits of Silas Baldwin/Sheriff's sale at suit of Robert Morgan: tract called Arabia Petre, 116 a.; also yoke of oxen, prop of Reubin Jones; also waggon, prop of James Jones; and 3 cows, prop of Joseph Jones/Sheriff's sale of right of John Sample to pt of Barnes Delight, Barnes Neglect, Barnes Neighborhood, Brother's Discovery, Maiden's Mount, the Plough and Union Fishery, at the suit of John Archer/Sheriff's sale at suit of David Kizer and Samuel Keyser, of right of Susquehanna Bridge Co to Bridge across Susquehanna called Conowingo Bridge - Samuel Bradford, Sheriff/Sale of James Kelley's at suit of Nathan Luffborough is postponed - Joshua Guyton, late sheriff/Sheriff's sale at suit of John Rumsey(?) at house of James Knight in Havre-de-Grace: tracts called Brother's Lot and Aquila's Inheritance, prop of Samuel Hughes/. Sheriff's sale at suit of John Archer and John W. Stump, use of executors of est of John Stump, 2 at suit of Hugh W. Evans, following lands: Addition to Brothers Lot, pt Martin's Ludgate, Lofflin's Neglect, Birchfield's Venture and many, many more tracts/I am now wanting, at North Hampton Furnace, a waggoner - J. Day, manager/Horses for sale - I. D. Henley

99. BUM Jul 25 1822/Sale by order of Orphans Court of pers prop of John Norris, decd - John Norris, adm/Preston M'Comas reports his sorrel horse strayed or stolen/Cook wanted - James W. Williams, nr Priest's Ford, Deer Creek/Four pairs of oxen for sale: James Reardan/Sheriff's sale at the suit of Theodore Delmas: pt of tract Belle Farm, being the dwelling plantation of

Isaac Wilson's; also negro Poll, 25; negro Abraham, 15; negro Frank, 10; negro George, 6/Sheriff's sale at suit of William W. Webster of negro Casandra, 5; negro Charles, 7; and furniture, prop of James Galloway /Sheriff's sale at suit of Rebecca Nowland of right of William Paca to tracts: Common Garden and pt of Mathews' Enlargement/Sheriff's sale at suit of John Webster adm of William Lester, agnst Hosea Barnes, of negro Spencer who has about 2 yrs to serve; negro Hager, 26 yrs of age; negro Henry, 2 yrs of age/Sheriff's sale at suit of John Evatt sen. of right of Nicholas Cox, Joseph H. Cox and Mary Cox to: pt of Onions Meadow Ground, Guffy's Delight, Johnston's Choice, Hutchinson's meadows and Guffy's Romantic Prospect, all lands conveyed by Israel Cox in his life time to said Nicholas Cox, Joseph H. Cox and Mary Cox/Wanted to purch by trustees of the Poor - a 200-300 a. farm - Benjamin Rigdon, Chairman

100. BUM Jul 28 1825/Sheriff's sale at suit of Susquehanna Bridge Co, use of Jacob Job: mare, horse, coalt, 2 cows, prop of Joseph Hopkins/Sheriff's sale of mare, prop of Harrison Stump - Henry H. Johns, Sheriff/Sheriff's sale at suit of John Wilson of mare, colt, prop of ___; also 2 yokes of oxen, prop of John T. Amos and 1 mare and 1 yoke of oxen of James Curry; also at suit of Havre-de-Grace Bank, negroes, Jim, Phill, Bil, Hampton, Sam, Frank, Susan, 3 mares, 3 horses, gig, a 4-horse wagon, 2 ox carts, about 500 bushels of wheat, prop of Edward Hall of Rumney; also at suit of Stevenson Archer: 1 waggon, mare, stack of wheat, ox cart, field of corn, prop of Kent Mitchell; also at suit of Jacob Lindenberger, surviving partner of George Lindenberger, tract called Strife, 53 a., negro men: Cope and Jack, prop of Thomas Ayres /Sheriff's sale at suit of James Guyton adm of John Guyton, negro boys: one 16, Nace age 12, Lewis age 10, 1 bay mare, 1 bay colt, 1 spotted mare, 1 yoke of oxen, ox cart, 2 lots of corn on the ground, 1 white cow, prop of William Wilson/Sheriff's sale of John Enlows adm of James Enlows, right of Thomas M. Enlows to one undivided ninth of 295 a., being parts of Charles Bounty, Charles Neighbor and Jones' Venture; also at suit of Thomas Ayres, right and interest of Agness Gordon to tract, Constable Manor and the Fragment, 71 a., 1 stack of rye and 1/3 pt of field of corn; also at suit of Thomas Ayers, right of William Amoss to land, 135 a., 1 yoke of oxen and mare and colt - Henry H. Johns, Sheriff

101. BUM Jul 28 1825/Late Sheriff's sale of right of Thomas Courtney Jr to parts of 2 tracts called Brown's Discovery and Rich Level, 350 a.; also parts of sundry tracts being the dwelling plantation of late Thomas Courtney sen., 257 a., negroes: Harry, 25; Hellen, 27; Delia, 23; Julian, 11; Nelly, 11; Susan 9; prop of Thomas Courtney sen; also at suit of Havre de Grace Bank, pt of tract, Fanny's Inheritance, 60 a., prop of Jonathan Sutton; also pt of tract Delph Farm, 388 a., prop of William W. Warner; also mare colt, oxen, horse, ox cart, prop of William M. Dallam and Francis J. Dallam exec of Josias W. Dallam; also right of John Love to lands, Great Britain, Robert's Lot and pt of one, name unknown, 159 a.; also tract, Arabia Petrea, owned by Elizabeth Murray/Sheriff's sale at suit of Levy Court of Harf Co, right of Abraham Jarrat to pt of Wild Cat Den, pt of Contestible Manor No. 2, 142 a. now in possession of Robert Fife, pt of Belle Grade, 2nd part No. 2, 100 a.; also in possession of Robert Fife, pt of Wild Cat Den, pt of Belle Grade No. 1 & 2 and pt Contestable Manor No. 1, 137 a., in possession of William Marshal, pt of Wild Cat Den and pt Bellee Grade, 14 a., in possession of James Watson; pt Belle Grade, 50 a., in possession of Nathan Yearly; also pt of Herman's

Addition and Betty's Lot, 62 a.; Triple Union and Friendship, 200 a.; and 1 grist mill/Sheriff's sale at suit of Elizabeth Bussey, right of Thomas Griffin to tract Bloom's Bloom, 135 a./Sheriff's sale at suit of John Johnson and Thomas Wilson, right of William Woolsey to tract, best Endeavour, 48 3/4 a./Sheriff's sale at suit of Richard Owens, right of Sally Wattars to plantation whereon late Stephen Watters decd formerly lived, 518 a./Sheriff's sale at suit of Elizabeth Birckhead, John Waters and James Reardan, admrs of Thomas H. Birkhead: negroes: Harry 32; Mariah, 27; Sam, 8; Ann, 6; being the goods and chattel of Mathew Dorsey, Harf Co, decd - Samuel Bradford, Late Sheriff

102. Jul 28 1825/Late Sheriff's sales: at suit of John Murphey, use of George Henderson, tract, Betsey's choice, 270 a., negro man, Stokes, 20; prop of Charles G. Hall/Late sheriff's sale at suit of state of Md, use of Charles McComas, right of Abner Gilbert to 90 a. whereon Abner Gilbert formerly lived /Late Sheriff's sale at suit of Thomas A. Hays, right of Solomon and Samuel Ady to tract, Friends Discovery, 14 1/4 a., pt of Colegate's Last Shift, 477 a.; prop of Henry Macatee/Late Sheriff's sale at suit of Andrew Porter Jr, use of John M. Dunn, negro woman Harriett, 25; prop of John Donn/Late Sheriff's sale at suit of Charles L. Bechme(?), pt of Billy's Portion, 83 a., pt of Widow's Garden, 92 a. and pt of Legs and Arms, 40 a.; prop of William Kennedy/Constable's sale at Dublin, right of Samuel Henry to Pleasant Plains; also right of Sedgwick James .....suit of William Lindsey - James Harvey, Constable. N. B. Sedgwick James' property was taken as security for Samuel Henry in the case/Constable's sale at suit of Francis J. Wheeler, right of Richard J. Wheeler to Wheeler's & Clark's Contrivance - Jehu Smith, Const. /Constable's sale at suit of William Richardson, right of Samuel Henry adm of Isaac Henry to Pleasant Plains/Flour Barrels wanted at Stafford Mills - Stump & Parker/Race will be run at Lewis Butler's Tavern, Upper Cross Roads - one saddle and briddle free for any horse in Balt or Harf Co/Tailoring - James Hackett, Darlington, recently from City of Balt/Officers of Extra Battalion to meet at Dublin - Frederick T. Amos, Major

103. BUM Jul 28 1825/Letters remaining at P.O. Havre de Grace: John Brown; Elizabeth Brooks; Z. O. Bond; Amos Cord; Aquila Donahoo; Capt William Dodson; Miss Susan Dallam; George Davis; Gilbert Gordon; Edward Griffith care of Dr. Norris; Benjamin Harris; William or Alexander Kerr; Patrick McKinley; Sarah Newell; James Russel..portion missing...- J. P. Bunting, Post master/Equity case - John Herbert vs Elihu B. Kennedy and others - sale of real est whereon James Kennedy lately lived - Stevenson Archer, trustee/Jonathan Matlack adm of John Smith vs John Smith and Eliza Smith, minors - sale of real est of John Smith/Commanding officers of troops attached to 7th Regt, Maryland Militia, to report to Commander of said Regt - John Streett, Colonel/Jesse Jarrett has just burnt a fresh kiln of lime; for sale/Jacob Gladden exec of John Alexander/Wool carding done at Abraham Jarrett's Mill - Peter Rodenhiser /John M. Donn has commenced saddle & harness making business in Havre de Grace/William D. Conway, M. D. late of U. S. Navy, offers his services at Pleasant Hils, lately owned by Edward Brinton nr intersection of Gunpowder and Belle Air Turnpike Road and adj former res of Dr. Bond/Jason Moore, surveyor/Nathan Ricketts insolvent debtor/R. N. Allen, Atty at Law, will attend in Bel Air every Tues/Rage of dysentery in Harf Co. Cabinet maker in Bel Air has made 60 coffins within a short time. In some families 3-4 deaths. In the family of James Kean on Sat last while the burial of a 2nd child was

taking place a third expired. Immediately in Belle-Air there have been but few deaths, which calls for thankfulness

104. Jul 28 1825/Unusually hot weather/John McFadden, tailor, has taken Henry Warren, late from Balt, in partnership, in Belle Air, next door to Mr. Hays Store/Sheriff's sale at suit of Thomas Ayres, right of Amelia Hitchcock to tract, name unknown, whereon she lives/Sheriff's sale of William F. Miller's prop postponed (at suit of John Forwood), use of Henry P. Ruff use of James Billingslea; also sale of John Donn's prop at suit of Lydia Barnes; also sale of Bennet Stewart's prop at suit of Edward Courtney exec of Jonas Courtney/Late Sheriff's sale at suit of Levy Court, right of Abraham Jarrett, formerly in possession of John Rockhold now in possession of Robert Richardson/Late Sheriff's sale at suit of Havre de Grace Bank, pt Strawberry Hills, 70 a., Lot No. 4, 67 a., Hall's Meadows, 128 a.; prop of Edward Hall; also negro women Jinny, 30; Sarah, 20; and negro girls, Susan, 11; and Ann, 8; prop of Edward Hall adm of Benedict Hall/Postponed sale of Isaac Wilson at suit of James Carroll/Thomas Wilson requests settlement of acccounts from his sale in Jan last/William S. Hays, Atty at Law, has taken up res in Belle Air /George M. Gill, Atty at Law/Otho Scott, Atty at Law, has removed to office next door to Parker Moore's Store/Equity case - Abraham Jarrett and Jesse Jarrett vs Francis Rockhold and Robert Richardson; bill states Francis Rockhold mortgaged to Abraham Jarrett 2 parcels of land; that Francis Rockhold does not now res in Md/Equity case - Jeremiah Brown vs Samuel Pyle, Daniel Pyle, John Pyle, Phebe Pyle, Joseph Pyle, Ruth Pyle and Orphia Pyle, heirs of Amos Pyle - sale of real est of Amos Pyle

105. BUM Jul 28 1825/Andrew Turk has just erected a new carding machine in the mill of James B. Preston on Deer Creek; he will receive wool at Edward Ringold's hatter's shop, Abingdon; George Cunningham's on road from Belle Air to Abingdon; William Richardson's, Belle Air; John Davis' tavern, Long Green, Blt Co/William B. Bond, Atty at Law has removed to office formerly occ by Mr. Scott and next door to Printing Office/John S. Lamburn and William Atherton have taken woolen factory and machinery formerly belonging to Daniel Lamburn nr Belle Air; wool will be rec'd at William Fitze's, William Bishop's on Belle Air road to Balt; Johnson's Mill (formerly Yellot's); Andrew Redden's nr the Hickory Tavern/William Gladden has purch a new carding machine; business will be conducted by John Johnson with long experience in the business; about 1/2 miles north of the Rocks of Deer Creek; fulling and dying also/James Run Woollen manufactory - William W. Forwood; wool will rec'd at Mr. Michael's, Cramberry Hill, Bush River Neck; Aquila Hall's Mill, Benum's Run; George Rider's, Hickory Tavern/John Sappington, M. D., res at Mrs. Bageley, Deer Creek and within a mile of Darlington, offers his services/Balt Camp meeting on land of John Worthington nr Randall's Town - Joseph Frye, Presiding Elder/Reuben Gilden to sell prop in Balt Co on Belle Air road, short distance from Abraham King's Tavern; also at dwelling of Mrs. Elizabeth Hughes, (to save the trouble of removal), some furniture/David Malsby sen., having concluded to remove to Deer Creek, offers for sale, prop in Bush Town: Tavern Stand which he occ many yrs and blacksmith shop and dwelling house /Constable's sale at suit of James Kennedy of right of William Amoss of James to tract, The Grove and 3 head of horses - John B. Foard, Constable

106. ICP Aug 14 1828/Rev Henshaw will preach at the Rock Spring Church/Died 11 inst at her res in Balt Co, Mrs. Priscilla Guyton in 84th yr/J. M. & T. C. Donn have opened in Havre-de-Grace a manufactory of coaches, gigs, pleasure carriages, saddles, harness, bridles &c./Sheriff's sale at suit of John Archer and John W. Stump, right of Clark Hollis to tract called Rumney Marsh/John McKenney, Jr and R. N. Allen, publishers of Independent Citizen, deny that Independent Citizen will become a "Caucus paper"/Dr. Allen feels it necessary to say that his editorial duties shall not be suffered in the slightest degree to interfere with his attention to practice, writing a few hours in each week, and visiting Bel-Air once during that period; the other affairs of the press are conducted entirely by Mr. McKenney/Letters remaining in P.O. Bel Air: Temperance Amos; Samuel Baxter; John Butler, care Rev T. O'brien; Jesse Car; John Cain, Sheriff; Lloyd Calder; Capt. Wm. Clark; Thos. Calwell; John Christopher; Dr. Conway; Mrs. Elizabeth Connelly; Mrs. Elizabeth Cain; Dr. Archd. Dorsey; Levy D..bo.; John England; Thos. Feincour, care Mr. S. Jones; Wm. or John Green; Mrs. Mary Greme; Thos. Green; B. Gilbert; Wm. Gladden; Wm. Hanway; David Harry; Nathl. Hollingsworth; Hannah Harlan; Josiah Johnson; C. D. W. Johnson; Benj. G. Jones, Esq.; Samuel James; Samuel A. Johnson; Thos. Kelly; Matthew Kennard; Thos. Lilly; Robt. Lyons; Wm. Michael; Andrew M'Adow; Mrs. Hannah Morris; David Morrison; John M'Nabb; Mrs. Sarah Morris; Wm. B. Montgomery; P. Moores; Dr. Jas. Montgomery; Vincent Norris; Wm. Nelson; David Newlin; Pr. Paper maker; Miss Sarah Preston; Stephen...; Miss Esther Rogers; Mrs. Margaret Richardson; Abm. Spicer; James Smith; Wm. Smithson; James Steel; John Slade; John Tredway; Alexander Tease; John C. Vaughan; Wm. Vink; Joseph E. Warner; Joseph Whitson; Josias Wilson; Solomon Wadlow; James, Nathaniel, Saml. or Mary Ann Whann, care of Glenn Street; Wm. Waterson; Miss Lydia Weiser - John McKenney, Jr. P.M

107. ICP Aug 14 1824/Harry D. Gough candidate for Commissioner/Albert Constable, Atty at Law in Bel-Air, occ office formerly occ by Judge Archer/Dr. Clarkson Freeman, of the city of Lancaster, Pa, has appointed T. A. & N. Hays, of Bel-Air, agents for the sale of the valuable medicine, Indian Specific/Sale by decree of Harf Co Court of real est in Harf co of late William Hanna which he died seized, being pt of two tracts: Good Neighborhood and Aquila's Inheritance, on road from Herbert's Cross Roads to Port Deposit Bridge - Thomas Jeffery, Samuel Bradford, Joseph Davis, John Robinson, Harry D. Gough, commissioners/Trustee's sale for the benefit of the creditors of William F. Miller, of negro boy named Gerard aged 13 to serve until 35; negro woman named Betsey aged 23, a slave for life; horses, cows, work oxen, sheep, hogs, farming utensils, household and kitchen furniture; right to plantation where William F. Miller now lives, 240 a.; also to be sold, 240 a. in ...Pa

108. ICP Aug 28 1828/New line of stages from Balt to Phila, passing through Bel-Air, Port Deposit Bridge, Brick Meeting House, New London Cross Roads, Kennet Square, Chads Ford, Concord Meeting House, Log Town, Wrangletown, Black Horse, Providence Meeting House, Gibbon's Tavern and Darby; leave Dr. Samuel B. Hugo's Tavern every Tues, Thurs and Sat about 12 o'clock/For sale - 20-30 sheep and 2-3 fresh calved cows - Joel Harry/Trustee's sale of five negroes, late the prop of Isaac T. Wilson, an insolvent debtor - L. D. Learned, Balt, trustee/Constable's sale at suit of Zepheniah Bayles adm of Mary Logan and at suit of Dr. William M. Dallam, at Nicholas Baker's store, right of Joseph Everet, tract whereon said Everet now res - James Stillings, Constable/Constable's sale, at suit of James Moores, surviving exec of Wakeman

Bryarly, right of Thomas Kelly to land where said Kelly now res; also lot of potatoes in the ground, lot of coopers' stuff, lot of barrels, two stacks of hay, one barrick of hay and one lot of oats - John Carsins, constable/Race at Havre-de-Grace for purse of $50 - Hall & Huggins/Joseph Davis candidate for County Commissioner for the 2nd Elect Dist/Dog lost or stolen - C. D. W. Johnson, Harf Co/Meeting of citizens of this county "friendly to the present Administration of the General Government." Joseph Davis called to the chair and William Worthington and James Wilson appointed secretaries. Meeting held at house of Dr. Saml. B. Hugo, in Bel-Air, on 12 Aug inst; address delivered by Augustus W. Bradford; few remarks by Dr. Jacob A. Preston; committee of correspondence: Beale Randall, Benj. C. Howard, Hugh McElderry, William Frick, Uptan S. Heath, Reverdy Johnson, Patrick Macauly, Richard Frisby, John P. Kennedy, Chas. C. Harper, Dabney S. Carr

109. ICP Aug 28 1828/Died Sat 23 inst, William D. Lee, one of the Judges of the Orphans' Court of this co, leaving large family/Dr. R. N. Allen has removed to Bel-Air, and occ stone house adj Mr. Hays' Store; patients at every distance will be attended with the strictest punctuality/John Hopkins and Robert Gover, of Philip, candidates for Commissioner for Dublin Dist/Col. Jacob Michael, candidate for Commissioner, for Hall's Cross Roads Dist/Daniel M. Cunningham and James Mather, candidates for Commissioners for Abingdon Dist/The 42nd Regt will parade at usual Parade Ground (Patterson's Field) with Arms and Accoutrements, in good order for Inspection. The General will Review the Regiment on that day, when and where the Colonel anticipates a full turn out of the Companies....- Henry Smith, Adjutant

110. ICP Sep 4 1828/Mahlon H. West declines candidacy/John Budd withdraws his candidacy for the Legislature/Married Tues last by Rev John R. Leech, Doct. Richard N. Allen, to Miss Adeline F. Miller, all of this co/The Extra Battalion will parade at Barclay's Old Field - F. T. Amos, Major/Labourers wanted to work on the Rail Road; enquire at Dr. Joseph Prigg's office, Eautaw st, opp Meth meeting house, Balt/James B. Amos, Harf Co, offers reward for negro man named Jacob Brown, about 5 ft 10 inch, about 43

111. ICP Sep 11 1828/Committee of Vigilance, to aid, by all fair and honorable means, in advancing the cause of the Administration, in this district..., William McCoy, Chairman; Michael Whiteford, Secretary: David Stokes; Jno. Scarbrough; Saml. Scarbrough; Harvey Stokes; Jno. Stokes; Wm. Elit; Joseph Albert; Jacob Balderson; Graftin Baker; John Caldwell; Chrs. Wilson, sen.; John Evatt, sen.; John Blackburn; Bradford Amos; John Allen; Simon Brown; Saml. Scarbrough; John Ingram; Hugh Jones; Wm. M'Nutt; Joseph Cherls; W. D. Smith; Wm. Wallace; Wm. Sullivan; Ephm. Hopkins; Jno. Hopkins; Saml. Hopkins; Joseph E. Hopkins; Wm. Worthington; Saml. Worthington; Hugh Smith, sen.; Hugh Smith, jun.; Jerry Harland; Henry Harland; Jno. Wakeland; Jas. Wilson; Jos. Stokes of David; Wm. Stump; Saml. Stump; Henry Stump; Lawson Gorrell; Robert Parker; Joseph Parker; Herman Stump; Chris. Wilson; Isaac Wilson; Saml. Way; Wm. Smith; John Qualls; Geo. Ewing; Joseph Wallis; Wm. Watson; Jno. Furguson; Wm. M'Jilton; Edw. J. Markland; William Eli; John Prevail; Jno. O. Bagley; Aquila Massey; Rigba Massey; Isaac Massey; Dr. Jno. Sappington; John Wiggins; Thos. Wiggins; Stephen Brown; Thos. Cunningham; Joshua Fleeharty; John How; Wm. How, sen.; Wm. How, jun.; Wm. Silver; Geo. Forsythe; David Troutner; Dew. Albett; Graftin Robertson; Elias Jones; James How; Wm. Forsythe; Joseph Jones; Joseph Forsythe; James Jones; John Jones; Lemen Jones; Richard Ward; Charles Ward; John Ward; Alex. Kerr; Joseph Rogers;

Saml. Rogers; Geo. C. Davis; Jos. Hopkins; Jas. L. Hopkins; James Lee; Chas. Lee, sen.; Chars. Lee, jun.; Jas. W. Williams; Elisha Johnston; Robt. Gover; James Gover; Edward Chew; Wm. Cole; James Cole; Saml. Hopkins; Joshua Hopkins; Levin Hopkins; Joseph Hopkins; John Fellen; Wm. Hopkins; Richd. Farmer; Wm. Farmer; Reuben Smith; Joseph More; George Harris; Jas. Scarbrough; Archd. Scarbrough; Joseph Jones; Asoph Warner; Thos. Warner; Joseph Warner; Silas Warner; James Healey; John Healey; Thos. M'Gomery; Michael Huff; Thos. Huff; Jesse Huff; Robert M'Gomery; Thos. Williamson; Jno. Williamson; Jesse Williamson; Wm. Miller; Wm. M'Nabb; Thos. M'Faddon; George Bagley; Jno. Burkins of Isaac; Parker Prigg; Wm. M'Coy, jun.; Joseph M'Coy; Nichs. H. Cox; Thos. Gillaspie; Wm. Gillaspie; Isaac Barnes; Saml. Kinade; Cungm. Whiteford; Archd. Heaps; John Heaps; Wm. Whiteford; Fred. T. Amos; N. S. Bemis; Jas. B. Amos; Chas. Lytle; Josiah Johnson; Thos. Wright; George Amos; Daniel Whiteford; David Eaton; Wm. Day; John Morrison; Thos. Proctor; Francis M'Atee; Amos Jones; James Johnson; Andw., Torbort; Hugh Whiteford; Aquila Amos; Thos. Demoss; Benj. Rigdon; John Butler; Wm. Fleeharty; George Rigdon; Alex. Rigdon;; Benj. Rigdan, jr.; Wm. Gladdin; Jacob Gladden; Wm. Wardan; Wm. Kennady; Jas. Dever of Richd.; Harman Dever of do.; George Dever of do.; John Jordan; Thos. Johnson; Phelix Herbert; Folger Pope; Nathan Pyle; David Pyle; Saml. Bevard; John Wright; Mark Wright; Jno. Wright of Thos. Wm. Rigdon; Ignatius Rutledge; Mathew Morrison; Ambrose Morrison; Elijah Jones; Joel Harry; Mordecai Thomas; Hugh Quigley; Hu. Whiteford of M.; Hu. Whiteford of W.; John M'Kenny; Isaac Harry; Wm. Addam; Wm. Adams; James Jones; Lloyd Heaps; James Guyton; Henry Fullard; Benj. Scarbrough; John Robertson; Horatio Miller; Maj. Robt. Morgan; Thos. Dever; Samuel Lee; John Brannon; James Wells; Silas Silver; John Harmer; Joseph Harmer; Joshua Harmer; Abrm. Harmer; Jas. Cunningham; Andw. Cunningham; James M'Nabb; Joseph H. Cox; John Galbreath; Robert Kerr; Edward Kerr; Abrm. Cavender

112. ICP Sep 11 1828/To bridge Builders - Levy Court of Harf Co will receive proposals for building two bridges: one over Gray's Run, on the Post road leading from Balt to Havre-de-Grace and the other over Binam's run, on the road leading from Bel-Air to the Lower Cross Roads. The bridge over Gray's run to be built of wood, and 30 ft in the clear; the abutments of stone, to be laid with lime and sand; roofed and weather-boarded. The bridge over Binam's run, to be of similar construction - Henry Dorsey, clk

113. ICP Oct 2 1828/Sale by order of Orphans Court of Harf Co of the pers est of Mary Bailey, decd: cows, furniture, 1 8-day clock, negro boy, at her late dwelling nr A. Gilbert's; also in Havre-de-Grace: 1 ten plate stove, 1 cherry tree cupboard, and other items - Amos Gilbert, Sen admr/Robert Gover, of Philip, denies that he cheated the Levy Court of Harf Co of $300/Henry Dorsey, Clk, Harf Co Levy Court, attests to the fact that the Justices of Levy Court levied sum of 37 pounds, 10 shillings for building bridge over the Gutter at Robert Gover's mill, which allowance was made payable to the said Gover; a suit was brought agnst him for a return on the same and a judgement obtained

114. ICP Oct 9 1828/For rent - That stand for business known by the name of Mount Vernon, on Post Road between Balt and Havre-de-Grace - John & Benj. W. Duncan; also 80 a. formerly prop of Joshua Day, decd, about 4 miles from Bush Town, and on the new road leading from Bush to Port Deposit Bridge/Sale of prop of William F. Miller for the benefit of his creditors is postponed /Examinatione at Bel-Air Academy to commence - John M'Kenney, Jr, Sec'ry /Saml. Bradford, auditor, requests creditors of Aquila Miles, Henry

Touchstone, and William M. Chew, Harf Co, decd, file their claims/Amos Waters adm of Benjamin Waters/ Third and fourth pages of this issue are missing

115. ICP Oct 16 1828/Commissioners elected:1st Dist - Francis Delmas; 2nd Dist - Jacob Michael; 3d Dist - Robert W. Holland; 4th Dist - John Smithson; 5th Dist - John Hopkins/Meeting of the friends of the National Administration will be held at house of James Knight in Port Deposit/For rent - farm on which James M'Claskey now res adj subscriber, Elizabeth Billinglea; also farm on road from Bel-Air to Rock Spring Church, at present occ by Bennet Love/Sale at res of George Allender nr Lee's Mill, remaining pers est of Nicholas Allender decd, consisting of negro girls, slaves for life - Benj'n Richardson, adm/Wanted a person to take charge of an English School - Jacob Michael, Michaelsvile, Rumney Neck

116. ICP Oct 16 1828/Letters remaining at P.O. Bel Air: Wm. Ashdown; Jas. Amos; Dr. R. H. Archer; John Blake; Jas. Bermingham; Elisha Bull; Lewis Butler; Benjamin Baxter; John Blaney; James Baker; Ebn'r Brown; Mr. Baxter (cooper); Saml. Cook; Miss Sarah E. Clendenin; Arch'd Culley; Mrs. Leon'd Clarkson; Dr. S. H. Coale; Wm. Cooper; Thos. Caldwell; Dr. Arch'd Dorsey; Mrs. Marg't Dagg; John D. Daugherty; Mr. Edward, care of J. Slee; Jas. Enlows; Mrs. Hester Ann Giles; Wm. Glenn; Chs. Gilder; John L. Griffith; Mrs. Hester Harkins; Maj. Henry Hall; Henry H. Jones; Miss Mary A. Jones; Stephen Jones; Saml. James; Jos. Joans; Dr. Jas. Johnson; Jas. Kenedy, Junr.; John Kean; John Lingum; Jas. Lytle; Hr. or Danl. Long; George Lemmon; Jesse Leake; Stewart Marshall; Elder Jas. G. Mitchell; Robt. McCrea; Morris Malsby; Ann Mason; Wm. Michael; John M. Leilson; Mrs. Sarah Norrington; Wm. G. Procter; Folger Pope; Edwd. Prigg; Mrs. Avarila J. Preston; Rachel Preston; Geo. Rider; John Rogers; Rowland Rogers; Mrs. Eliz. St Clair; James Smith; Abm. Street of David; Rogers Street; Henry Scarf; John Slee; James Sherdin; Harvey Stokes; Miss Margaret Sheed, care of E. Litle; Wm. Temple; Wm. P. Welch; Josias Wilson; James Whitaker; Mrs. Letitia Wilson; Wm. H. Wilson; Mrs. Mary Waters; Mrs. Jane Ward; Wm. Watt - John McKenney, Jr P.M./La Mott's Cough Drops - T. A. & N. Hays, Belle-Air

117. ICP Oct 23 1828/Major Henry S. Stites at Port Deposit is authorized to receive subscriptions for Indepedent Citizen/Rev Slicer will preach in Court House/Constable's sale at suit of Richard Mitchel adm of Sarah Benett and at suit of Richard Mitchel at George W. Hall's in Havre-de-Grace, right of James Hughes to tract where John Botts res/Constables sale at suit of William Sappington, right of James Hughes to tract where John Botts now res /Constable's sale at suit of William Sappington, of right of James Mahon to tract within 1 1/2 miles of Mudtown, being tract where Sarah Mahon now res - James Stillings, constable

118. ICP Nov 6 1828/Constable's sale at the suit of Peter and Jacob Hoopman, and suit of James Moores, right of Aquila Osborne to land whereon said Aquila Osborne now res/John B. McFadden, tailor, has removed to new house opp entrance to Alexander Hannas' farm/Married Tues 14 ult by Rev John Goforth, Rev William Ryder of Kent Co, Md, to Miss Rachel Davis, of Harf Co/Equity case - William S. Hays, Charles Mitchell and John Saunders vs Charlton Waltham and Hester his wife; Robert Banker Saunders; William Saunders; John Saunders; and Margaret Saunders. Bill of complaint states that Robert Saunders, decd, in his life time was indebted to the plaintiffs but died around 20 Nov 1825; that William S. Hays and Charles Mitchell, two of the complaintants upon a suit

instituted agnst Mary Saunders the administratrix of said Robert for the recovery of their claim aforesaid, recovered judgment for $100. Robert Saunders died seized of pt of a tract called Jones Inheritance, 160 a., leaving following children: Robert Banker Saunders, William Saunders, John Saunders and Margaret Saunders, all of whom res out of the state of Md, and it is belived they are in state of New York. Robert Banker Saunders has, since death of his father, conveyed his interest to Hester Waltham, wife of Charlton Waltham, who res in this co/Sale of furniture, farming utensils, oxen, cattle, blacksmiths tools, and other items - John & Benjamin W. Duncan, Mount Vernon, Harf Co/Constable's sale at suit of John Archer, at suit of William B. Bond use of Ephraim Lytle, at suit of William Sappington, at suit of Richard Mitchel adm of Sarah Bennet, at suit of Richard Mitchel, of right of James Hughes to tracts Friendship and Eigh Trap, 100 a.

119. ICP Nov 13 1828/Executor's sale by order of Orphan's Court of Harf Co at former rs of Buckler Bond, nr Bel-Air, part of pers est of Wm. D. Lee, decd - James Moores, Joshua Wilson, exec

120. ICP Nov 20 1828/Sale by order of Harf Co Court of the prop of Wm. Tucker, decd - Js. Wetherall, Ths. Dorney, Wm. Thomas, Commissioners/Lost - a hound dog - William Richardson

121. ICP Dec 18 1828/Equity Court-Robert Morgan vs John Jolly, surviving adm of William Jolly decd; bill of complaint states that John Jolly and John Wallis as adm of William Jolly decd recovered judgment agnst the complainant which were paid; states the death of one of the administrators, and plaintiffs, and that John Jolley the survivor res out of state of Md; that payments made be allowed/John L. Gibson and Miles Hilton, Harf Co, late imprisoned debtors of Harf Co/New Goods - Amos Smith/James W. Williams, Preistford, Deer Creek, wants to hire farm hand/Sale of stock of goods in the store at Conowingo Corner - Joseph Miles, Jr/Constable's sale of right of James Harvey to tract whereof Elizabeth McFadden now res, adj lands of John McFadden and Isaac Hawkins, at suit of Dr. John Sappington - John S. Ward, constable/Sale on farm occ by Amos Cord, in Bush River Neck, adj those of John Chauncey and W. T. Hall, of rye, oats, hay horses, being part of pers est of William D. Lee, decd - James Moores, Joshua Wilson exec of William D. Lee/Excellent account of Battle of Balt in War of 1812/For sale at his farm in Rumney Neck nr Michaelsville, his entire stock of horses, cattle, sheep, hogs, farming utensils, four yoke of oxen well broke, 2 ox carts, 1 horse cart, corn fodder and husks and other articles - Nathaniel Sillick/Jacob Michael forwarns persons from receiving note of hand payable to Henrietta Gallion of state of Indiana for $276

122. ICP Dec 25 1828/No new items

123. ICP Jan 1 1829/James W. Williams, Preistford, candidate for congress, from 6th Congressional Dist/Sale of lands in Gunpowder Neck, late the prop of William Tucker decd postponed - Thomas Dorney, James Wetherall, William Thomas, Commissioners

124. ICP Jan 8 1829/Married in Balt on 1 inst by Rev Morrison, William C. Vance to Miss Mary Wiley, dau of Matthew Wiley, all of Harf Co/Farm in Harf Co for sale containing 500 a., about 1 mile from Little Falls of Gunpowder and 1 miles form Joppa - Col. Edward A. Howard, within 3 miles of farm /Letters

-34-

remaining at P.O. Bel-Air: Edwd F. Bussey; Zachariah Bond; Josiah Brown; Messrs. Henry & Briddle; Nathan S. Bemis; Mrs. Elizabeth M. Brown; Capt. Wm. Clark; Archibald Culley; Mrs. Matthew Cain; Wm. Carr, Jr; Edith Cheyner; Robert Chapel; Dr. A. Dorsey; Levi Denbow; John England; Miss Lydia Forwood; Samuel Foreman; Thomas Griffin; Joshua Guyton jr; Wm. Gladden; Robt. T. Henderson; Nicholas Hackett; Thos. Hope; John Henderson; Jos. Hart; Wash. Hanway or broths.; Miss Mary L. Hughes; Thos. Hanway; Capt. C. D. W. Johnson; Mrs. Jane Johnson; H. Johns; Rebecca James; Mrs. Sarah Johnson; Stephen Jones; Jabez Kirkwood; Edward Kerr; William Kelly; Benjamin Lukens; James McFadden; Elder James McVey; Miss Elizabeth McFadden; Mrs. Mary Mackey; Thos. Montgomery; Dr. James Montgomery; David Maulsby; Hannah Morrison; J. H. Munnickhuysen; Midm. J. H. Maulsby; Alexr. Noris; Vincent Norris; Luther A. Norris; Geo. Plumly; Elder Wm. G. Proctor; Mrs. E. A. Preston; Mrs. Hannah Ruff; Rev John Robb; Jesse Rockhold; Mrs. Richard Richardson; James Rampley; Wm. Rigdon; Miss Jane W. Rutledge; ___Rider; Maj. Wm. Richardson; Alexander Spicer; Wm. Sawyer; James Sheridine; Thomas Scott; Wm. Smithson; Miss Renis Smithson; James Stephenson; Thomas Tredway; Caleb Wright; James Whitaker; John Watkins; Geo. H. Wilson - John McKenney, Jr - P.M.

125. ICP Jan 15 1829/Store-house, together with stock of goods, belong to Edward J. Markland, of Darlington, consumed by fire; fire was discovered between 3 and 4 o'clock in the morning/Married Tues 6 inst by Rev Park, John L. Johnson, to Miss Levinia Michael/Married Thurs 8th by same, William Ward to Miss Mary Ann Grafton/Died Thurs last in 18th yr of her age, Miss Elizabeth Hutchins, 3rd dau of William Hutchins of this co/Died Mon last, Aquilla Grafton aged 72/Died in Balt 3 inst, after a long and painful ill- ness, Jason Brown Downer, aged 27, native of Vermont/Land for sale being part of real est of Thomas Butler decd and adj lands of Colonel John Street - Lewis Butler/Sale at Swan Creek: horses, oxen, cows, steers, hogs, horse wagon, ox cart, farming utensils, furniture, stove and other articles - Joseph Brownley

126. ICP Feb 5 1829/Sale at his res: horses, cows, horse cart, ploughs, harrows, grain, furniture, 3 stoves, white oak flooring and other plank and other articles - Charles D. W. Johnson, Liberty Mills/James Garrison cautions that his wife Susannah Garrison, late of Harf Co, but now of city of Balt, has conducted herself improperly by the continued use of spirituous liquors; he shall not pay any debts of her contracting from this date/Farm for sale where he now res - John Chauncey/Sheriff's sale of right of Benjamin G. Jones to tract called French's Lot, 107 1/2 a. - Jason Moore, late sheriff to satisfy suits of state of Md/Sheriff's sale of right of John Street to tract Better Luck, 307 a. to satisfy suit of state of Md/Sheriff's sale of right of Thomas Ayres to tract called Smith's Still, 140 a., to satisfy two judgments at the suit of state of Md/Sale of pers est of Margaret Ely decd - Joseph Saunders, adm

127. ICP Feb 26 1829/Boarders wanted - The misses Scott, at their res 1 mile from Bel-Air/Sheriff's sale of tract called Abraham's Inheritance, prop of Edward Kerr at suit of James Stephenson; also farm on which Edward Kerr res at suit of Robert Taylor/Snow storm on 20th; the average depth was 10-11 inch, enormous drifts/On 4 Feb David McLaughlin was shot to death by John Taylor Kid, nr the mouth of Octorara creek, Cecil Co; a reward of $100 has been offered for the apprehension of Kid/Died Tues 3 inst after a short illness, Mary B. Brown, in 73d yr/John Grafton requests creditors of Aquila Grafton decd to present claims/Sheriff's sale of prop of Thomas Ayres: Strife Angle,

Old Man's Meadows and Ditch Meadows and other tracts, at suit of Hugh McElderry, James Gladden, Peter Dincle, and state of Md, use of William H. Stump use of Edward Griffith/Sheriff's sale of prop of Dixon Slade: Russel's Chance and Slade's Charm at suit of James Gladden; Sheriff's sale at suit of Lydia Barnes, of prop of John Hanson: Drew's Enlargment/Sheriff's sale at suit of Lydia Barnes: 8 head of horses, prop of James McGaw/Sheriff's sale at suit of Nathan B. Hammond, use of David Stewart, prop of Wm. McJilton: Dunkard's Harbor and Mary's Lot, 4 a., 1 shad seine, 1 batteaux, 1 feather bed, 1 wagon, and 1 spotted cow/Sheriff's sale of tract Robinhood's Forest, prop of Mary Bailey, at suit of Daniel Smith/Sheriff's sale of prop of Luther Smithson of land adj land of Edward Smithson, 111 a., at suit of state of Md /Sheriff's sale of prop of John Love: Great Britain, Robert's Lot at suit of state of Md/Sheriff's sale of tract, Convenience, 30 a., in possession of Benj. Hobbs, terre tenant of Samuel Hughes, at suit of John Archer & J. W. Stump, use of John Stump's executors

128. ICP Mar 5 1829/The large ox raised and fed by William M. Lansdale of this co has been sent to Balt; he measures from nose to rump, 13 ft 6 inch; height 6 ft 6 inch; girth 8 ft 9 1/2 inch; shoulder to dewlap 5 ft 1/2 inch /The Rev Messrs. Jennings and Sneden are expected to attend the Quarterly meeting at Calvary Church of the Associated Meth Church/Hay for sale - Stevenson Archer, Thomas A. Hays, admrs of Archer Hays/Sheriff's sale of mare, horse and calf, prop of Jacob Forwood of John, at suit of Saml. Bradford/Prop for sale : 15 1/2 a. with dwelling house, store house, ware house, hatters shop, stable and wagon house adj Little Falls Friends Meeting House lot - Aaron Patterson

129. ICP Mar 12 1829/Married Tues evening last, by Elder McVey, Andrew Gordon to Miss Elizabeth England, both of this co/Died at Blenheim, res of Paca Smith, on 6 inst, Mrs. Martha Phillips, widow of late James Phillips, senr. of Harf Co, at age of 85; for some time prev to death, she was afflicted with bodily disease/Died Tues evening 10 inst, Elisha Rutledge, 24-25 yrs old, married but a few months, victim to the small pox/Land for sale at William Pyle's Saw Mill, tract known as William's Discovery, within 3/4 mile of ore bank belonging to Evan T. Ellicot; call on subscriber, in Broad Creek, Harf Co - Nathan S. Bemis/From causes which are not necessary to be detailed here, but which are known to my neighbours, the usual preaching which has been held regularly at my house on the 4th Sabbath of May annually, for several years, will be discontinued - Amos Jones

130. ICP Mar 19 1829/Harf Co Court results of spring term: State vs Negro Moses Anderson for indictment for larceny, unable to reach verdict; State vs Edward M'Cartney, indictment for larceny, guilty, sentenced to the penitentiary for 2 yrs; State vs George Woolley, indictment for larceny, verdict guilty, sentenced to penitentiary for 2 yrs/Died Tues 10 inst, Wm. Woolsey /Died Sat last, Walter Bull, at an advanced age/Died same day, Clement Green /Sale of pers est of Benjamin Rigdon, Harf Co, decd by Alexander Rigdon, agent for Elizabeth Rigdon, adm of decd/Farm for sale whereon he res - Charles G. Hall/Cranberry Mill is for sale, including 50 a., two dwellings, store house, corn house, tan-yard lately sunk, with currying shop, grist and saw mill - Gerard Mitchell

131. ICP Mar 26 1829/Married Wed 18 inst by Rev John R. Keech, Oliver H. Amos of Harf Co to Miss Elizabeth Ann, only dau of Abram King, of Balt Co /Married

Thurs 12 inst by Rev Parke, John Mitchell, to Miss Agnes Edgar, all of York Co, Pa/Died 20 inst, Miss Ellen Green of this co, only child of her parents; her father died about a week before/Dr. J. Gillett has settled at Herbert's Cross Roads, and will be found at the house of Mr. Hanna/Farm for sale upon which William Amos of James now res, 241 a., on Winters'Run - Albert Constable, trustee/Farm on Winters' Run for rent - Samuel R. Smith, Balt/Mercer potatoes for sale - J. McKenney, Jr, Bel-Air/No small pox reported in Harf Co since that reported in Independent Citizen on the 12th inst/The ship Elvira, bound from St. Augustine to Norfolk, suffered shipwreck on Sat 21 Feb. Some of the persons on board, after remaining on the wreck nearly 3 weeks, were taken off by Captain Glover, of the schooner Milo, and conveyed to Newport, Rhode Island. William H. Allen, formerly of this co, was one of those taken off by Captain Glover.

132. ICP Mar 26 1829/Orphan's Court: John Forwood, John Norris, Thomas A. Hays; Coroners: John McKenney, William Richardson, Robert Bradford; Surveyor: Jason Moore; Justices of the Peace: George Bradford, James Steel, William Smith of Samuel, Joseph Worthington, Dr. Elijah Davis, William Allen, William Glenn, Hosier Barnes, Wm. Sheckle, Walter T. Hall, Jacob Michael, Stephen Waters, Zephaniah Bayless, Benjamin Silver, Henry G. Waters, James M'Gaw, Goldsmith Day, James Moores, Ebenezer N. Allen, John Donn, William Silver, Stephen Jones, Samuel Bradford, Robert Richardson, Joseph Renshaw, Platt Whitaker, Joseph Davis jr, John Smithson, George Griffith, H. Wilson, Edw'd Kerr, Timothy Kean, John Wiley, Roger Street, James Wetheral, Francis Delmas, James S. M'Comas, Amos Waters, James Bond Preston, James Lytle, Michael Whiteford, Vincent Norris, Jacob Bradenbaugh, Abel Watkins, Danl. Wann, Saml. Brown, Thomas G. Howard, James Wilson, John Hopkins, Jas. B. Amos, Harry D. Gough, Winston D. Smith, Thomas H. Gillespie, Thomas Caldwell jr, John W. Rutledge, Josiah Johnson, Samuel Reed, Robert Henderson, Jacob Hoopman, James Alexander, John Evatt jr, John Galbreath, William Vance, Benjamin Richardson, James Luckey, Nathan S. Bemis, Charles D. W. Johnson, Stephen Boyd, Ralph Clark, John C. Norris, William Cairns, John Duncan, Jefferson McCausland, Clement Butler, James W. Tolley, Bennet Doran, George Wareham, Rhesa Norris, Mahlon West, Francis E. Monks, John C. Forwood, James P. Gover, and Thomas C. Stump.

133. ICP Apr 16 1829/Letters remaining at P.O. Bel-Air: Miss Mary Ashdown; Thomas Ayres; Mrs. Temperance Amos; John Amos; James Amos; Elizabeth Amos; Reuben Allen; Miss Elizabeth Bay; Jas. M. Bay; Mrs. Sarah Bell; David Bell; Davis S. Brown; Elizabeth Brown; John Barclay; William P. Beal; John Clendenin; Nicholas Cooper; Edith Cheyney; commissioners of the Tax; Dr. A. Dorsey; Ann Denbow; Hy. Dorsey; John Elderkin; Edmund Evans; Jacob Fored; Henry Foy; Moses Foster; Elizabeth Fisher; Jacob Forward; D. Flours; A. I. Greme; Wm. Grafton; Wm. Green; Abm. Gibson; Joseph Harkins; Michael Huff; Amos Hoopes; James Huggins; Wm. Harrod; Miles Hilton; Mrs. Mary Harry; John Harvey; Mrs. Sane Johnson; H. H. Johns; Thos. Jeffery, Jr; Stephen Jones; Benj. G. Jones; Mrs. Johnson, care of Mrs. Brown; Josiah Johnson; Wm. Jourden; C. D. W. Johnson; Thomas Kain; Richard H. Kean; John Magness; Jacob Minnick; David Morrison; Job Mitton; Morris Malsby; Hy. G. Maynadier; Hugh McCown; ___McBlair; John McGaw, of Robt.; Thos. McClure; Saml. McGaw; Mrs. Hannah Patterson; M. H. Price; Saml. Parkinson; James Poteet, care of Otho Scott; Philip Ritcherdson care Mr. Griffith; Wm. Rutledge; John Renshaw; Ruth Renshaw; Isaac Robertson; Rowland Rogers; Elisha Rutledge; Col. Wm. Smith; Wm. Stump; Miss Ellen Sherding; James Smith; Robt. Stewart; Miss Julia Slade; David

Street; Rogers Street; Aquilla Thompson; Thos Tredway; Mrs. Martha Thompson; Danl. Wann; J. P. Waters - John McKenney, jr, Post Master

134. ICP Apr 16 1829/500 bushels of corn for sale - George Griffith/Oxen wanted to purchase - Robert H. Archer/Post Boy (horse) will be offered to the public for the ensuing season at the following stations: John Galbreath's; David Bell's; Samuel Watkin's, Long Green - John Fickey/Young Arab (horse) will stand at Capt. Brown's, Bush; Col. Michael's store, Hall's Cross Road and at subscribers, John Chauncey/Farm for sale on the Cranberry called Woodley Cottage, 150 a., 1/2 mile from Spesutia Church, adj farm of Isaac Perryman - Cordelia Giles, Blenheim/For rent - dwelling house on road from Hickory Tavern to Parker's mill adj lands of John Forwood - William Michael /Commissioners of Harf Co will meet - R. Richardson, clk/Election of 5 directors of Havre-de-Grace Ferry Company - George Bartol, Treasurer /Appointments for Balt Meth Conference: Northumberland Dist, David Steele, P.E.: Shamokin - Edward E. Allen; Northumberland - James W. Dunnahay, Josiah Forrest; Lycoming - William Prettyman, Charles Kalbfus; Belletfonte - Samuel Ellis, James H. Brown; Philipsburgh - Oliver Ege; Huntingdon - Jesse Collins, James Sanks; Lewistown - Amos Smith; Concord - Jonathan Munroe, Henry Tarring - - Carlisle Dist: John Baier, P.E.: Carlisle - Charles A. Davis; Carlisle Circuit - Jacob R. Shephard, Joseph Sprigg; A. Griffith, Supernumerary; York - Henry Smith, James W. Brent; Harford - Thomas McGee, John Poisal; Great Falls - Henry Slicer, George G. Brooks; Liberty - James Riley - George Hildt; Frederick - John A. Gere, Francis A. McNeil; Hagerstown - Edward Smith, B. D. Higgins; Chambersburg - Andrew Hemphill; Gettysburg - Samuel Keper, John C. Lyon; Thomas J. Dorsey, Seminary Agent; John A. Henning without an appointment at his own request; Robert H. Jordan transferred to Illinois

135. ICP Apr 16 1829/Dr. Mechem has removed to Bel-Air, next door to the office of Wm. B. Bond/John McKenney, Jr, having been removed from the office of Post Master at this place, it is now necessary that all those indebted to me for postage, should make immediate payment - John McKenney, Jr - (to make room for a friend of President Jackson, John Robinson)/Sale of horses, cows, sheep, hogs, farming utensils - Nicholas Cooper/Horse, Young Bacchus will stand at Wm. Richardson's, Bel-Air; Joseph Parker's mill on Deer Creek; James Bond, Preston's mill; Samuel Watkin's, Long Green - John Jervis/Imperial Sportsman will stand at Saml. Forwood's, nr Deer Creek; Mr. Ely's, Darlington; Isaac Richardsons, West Nottingham, Cecil Co - John W...

136. ICP Apr 23 1829/Married Tues evening last by Rev Benjamin Richardson, Israel Atkinson to Miss Hester Lancaster, all of this co/Dr. Bussey has removed to Nathan S. Bemis's on Broad Creek/Doctors R. H. Archer & Hopkins have associated themselves in the practice of Physic/Farm for sale in that highly improved vale leading to the mouth of Deer Creek, valuable sawmill, head and fall of water 20 ft; also farm on Long Green, in Balt Co; enquire of John Slee living on the farm in Harf Co or Thomas A. Hays living in Bel-Air or John Nicholson & Son brokers in Balt or subscriber living on the farm on Long Green - Joseph Slee/George Griffith, Jacob A. Preston, adm of John Hanson/Trustee's sale of tract in Gunpowder Neck whereon Thomas J. Calwell now res called Merrikens Inheritance Forever, 344 a. - John Tagart, trustee

137. ICP Apr 30 1929/Appointments: Justice of the Peace for Harf Co - James McConnell, Samuel Ady; 40th Regt, Harf Co: Augustus W. Bradford, Adjutant, vice Johns decd; Extra Battalion Harf Co: Winston D. Smith, Captain, vice Wilson resigned; Robert McCausland, Quarter Master/Married evening of 23 inst by Rev Finlay, Joseph Hanway of this co, to Miss Eliza Lindsey, of Balt City /Sale made by Samuel Bradford, trustee in the case of Thomas Kell agnst Caleb M. Hipkins confirmed/Sale of dwelling house and store in Faun Township, York co, Pa, 1/2 a.; apply to Wm. Vansant, living nr the prop or subscriber in Bel-Air, Samuel B. Hugo/To my creditors - I am extremely sorry that it is not in my power to meet the claims agnst me...I pledge to pay as soon as I can - Jacob Mitchell, Anne Arundel Co/Joseph Howard insolvent debtor, discharged from imprisonment

138. ICP May 7 1829/Severe criticism of President Jackson's rewarding offices and positions to political friends/Married Tues evening last, by Rev John R. Keech, Thomas Penniman, Merchant of Balt City, to Miss Delia M., second dau of Walter T. Hall, of this co/Died Mon last at her res on Deer Creek at an advanced age, Mrs. Hannah, consort of John Forwood

139. ICP May 14 1829/Died 27 ult at the res of his son in thic co where he was on a visit, Peter Hoke of York Co Pa, in 59th Rt/Rev Eli Hinkle will preach in Bel-Air on Sabbath morning and at William Wafters in the afternoon /Abraham Martin, insolvent debtor of Harf Co, to be disch from imprisonment /Trustees's sale of tract on Broad Creek, 100 a., late the prop of Israel Cox, and by him conveyed to Joseph D. Cox; grist and saw mill and dwelling house/Farm for sale on which William Coale lately res, adj lands of Messrs. John Norris and Nicholas M. Bond, 200 a. - Joshua Wile, within one mile of Bel-Air, where two of the most flourishing Academies (male and female) in the State are located - Joshua Wiles

140. ICP May 28 1829/Measles prevalent in this village, but we believe there are no cases attended with danger/White pine lumber, 50,000 feet seasoned plank, from one to two inch thick - James McConkey, Peach Bottom/Grain for sale - 50 bushels of corn, 20 bushels of rye - Phillip Rodenhiser at Aquilla Hall's mill - George Wm. Hall/Sheriff's sale of tract called Gilbert's Pipe, 50 a., and tract called Montreall, 50 a., and furniture, of Henry R. Gilbert, at suit of Ann Gilbert adm of Shadrick R., Gilbert/Sheriff's sale on the premises, tracts: Claxton's Forest, 203 a.; Three Sisters, 106 a.; negro girl aged 14 and other items

141. ICP Jun 4 1829/Mahlon H. West candidate for Gen Assembly/Trustee's sale of tract on Rumney Creek called Matthew's Enlargment, 360 a., being farm upon which Leonard Howard now res - Albert Constable, trustee/Richard D. Lee reports sheep strayed from his farm which adj Boothby Hill

142. ICP Jun 11 1829/Dr. Allen having retired fromthe editorial department of this paper, is succeeded by Augustus A. Bond/Death of Parker H. Lee on evening of 6 ult, during 71st yr of his age, native of this co, an officer in 5th Regt of Maryland line during the war of our Revolution (long obit.)/Died Sabbath evening last, Elizabeth Glassgow, dau of late Dr. James Glassgow, in 13th year of her age/Dr. James Montgomery, supported as candidate for legislature of Md/Camp meeting will be held for Great Falls Circuit on the land of Philip Moore, nr Long Green/Fulling, carding & manufacturing of cloth at Smith'sFactory - Robert W. Smith, agent

143. ICP Jul 16 1829/A violent storm passed over this village last Wed/Wheat crop if good; rye was much injured by the severity of the winter; the late rains have revived the oats, which now promise to be abundant; corn looks well/ Camp meeting to be holden on the land of Henry Webster, nr Calvary Meeting House - Eli Hinkle, min; Henry Webster, steward/Camp meeting for Harf Circuit nr Deer Creek Chapel - Thomas McGee, preacher in charge/Sale at suit of Susquehannah Bridge and Bank co of tract belonging to Amos Silver, called Mary's Lot, 300 a.; also right of Abner Gilbert to tract whereon he now lives, 90 a., at suit of State of Md, use of Charles McComas/Sheriff's sale of tract called Amos & Myers' Puzzle, 85 a., Baldwin's & Ashton's Innocence, prop of Thos. Ayres, adm of Thos. Daily, at suit of Martha Daily; also tract called Toland's Reserve, prop of Adam Toland, at suit of Benjamin Toland, Jr; also right of James Hughes, to tract called Friendship, 95 a., at suit of state of Md, use of John Archer; also sale of prop of Sarah James adm of Sedgwick James, at suit of Thos. Kell is postponed

144. ICP Jul 23 1829/Distressing accident - During the storm yesterday evening, a sail boat containing nine persons, was capsized in the river, between Whetstone Point and Harris's Creek. The boat is said to have sunk as soon as she went over, and six of the number were drowned. The occurrence was witnessed by several persons at Littlejohn's tavern, two of whom, Messrs. Geo. W. Ellis, and George Leary, put off in a very small boat, and by great exertions succeeded in picking up three of the men belonging to the sail boat. The extreme smallness of the boat prevented them from taking in any more. The men who were picked up reported the names of the lost companions to be - Thomas Solden, Richard Smith and his son, a lad of eight or nine years, James Tezin, Thomas Baggot, and James O'Connor - Balt. American /Married Thurs evening 16 inst by Rev Keech, Silas Silver to Miss Eliza Hanway, all of this co/Died in Balt Fri last, Charles Ridgely of Hampton late Governor of Md, in 70th yr

145. ICP Jul 30 1829/Died in this village Sun evening last, after a short illnes, Vincent Jeffery, in 45th yr/William Fulford seeks to employ servants /Wm. G. Shaw, living in Middle River Neck, Balt co, offers reward for black man who calls himself Basil Newton, but is commonly called Jacob; about 5 ft 4 inch, 33-34 yrs of age, thick set/Dry goods and grocers - Jacob H. Munnikhuysen, Samuel Gover, in Bel-Air

146. ICP Aug 6 1829/Frederick Taylor Amos candidate for Gen Assembly/William B. Stephenson candidate for Gen Assembly/Statement regarding conflict in dates of camp-meetings - Eli Henkle, Rhesa Norris, Benj. Richardson, Harf Co/Editor comments by Abrm. Jerrett, Mount Friendship/Death of Mrs. Harriet Forwood, consort of Dr. Parker Forwood, on Sat evening last/Partnership of Geo. Griffith and John W. Smith; business to be carried on by John W. Smith

147. ICP Aug 13 1829/Letter from Col. Mitchell nr Elkton, to Col. Little, Trustee's sale of farm lately in the possession of John W. Carlisle, consisting of pts of tracts, Fanny's inheritance, Raily and Middleborough - William F. Giles, trustee/Nicholas Cooper to sell furniture, milch cows and colt/Benjamin B. Amoss, wishing to leave the state, offers for sale lot occ as a tavern, formerly known by the name of Marshall's and is the place where the election of the 4th Dist is held and also the post office/Isaiah Cooper, Conowingo, has terminated his connexions with the store in which he had long been engaged and taken the store house lately occ by Mr. Miles/Thomas Johnson

nr Bel-Air, offers reward for colored woman named Jane, about 5 ft 8-9 inch, 31-32 yrs of age, broad face; she took with her a female child about 10 months old/Teresa Wheeler offers reward for negro woman named Julia or Julian, about 19, 5 ft 5-6 inch, proportionably large, formerly prop of Clement Green, late of Harf Co, decd; she has relations in Pennsylvania/Dr. R. N. Allen intends to res permanently in Bel-Air, where he will devote his undivided attention to his professional pursuits

148. ICP Aug 20 1829/James Moores candidate for Md legislature/Married Tues evening last by Rev Keech, James Lytle, Jr to Miss Mary McMath, all of this co/Thomas W. Bond has returned to Abingdon, at his old stand, where he has on hand, and intends keeping, a general assortment of Dry Goods & Grocers/Joshua Guyton candidate for sheriff of Harf Co/John Ferguson, Darlington, reports runaway indented apprentice to the Boot and Shoe making business named Joseph Fry, 19 yrs of age about 5 ft 6 inch, dark eyes, and dark hair; he wore fur hat, blue roundabout, Marseilles vest, white drilling pantaloons, white stockings, and pumps

149. ICP Aug 27 1829/The 40th Regt of Maryland Militia will parade nr Coop Town, (in the field where it met last year) with arms and accoutrements in good order, and provided with eight rounds of blank cartridges, for exercise, inspection and review. Captains Brown, Rutledge, and Streett, with their troops of Cavalry, are respectfully invited to unite with the Regiment in the manoeuvres of the day. By order of the Colonel, A. W. Bradford, Adjt, 40th Regt/Woollen manufactory at their establishment nr Nathan S. Bemis' mills where if they are favored with custom, hope to be able to manufacture fine and coarse cloths, flannel, kersey, linsey, blanketing - Aseph Warner, Harf Co

150. ICP Sep 3 1829/Died at res of her sister, in this co, Mon last, Mrs. Margaret Barney, consort of John H. Barney, of Balt City/Died Fri 21 ult, Alexander Sutherland, aged 80 yrs, a soldier of the Revolution/Died Thurs 27 ult, after a short but severe illness, Hugh Porter, aged 60 yrs/Died in city of Balt on Sun evening, 23 ult, after a protracted illness of several months, Dr. John Beale Davidge, professor of Anatomy in the Univ of Md/Mary Lee adm to sell pers est of Parker H. Lee/Equity case - Charles D. W. Johnson vs Nathan Walton, Joel Carter, John Woods and Avid Woods; bill of complaint states that John and David Woods around 1816 being seized in fee of a tract in Harf Co called Bond's Last Shift, either bartered or sold same to said Joel Carter; bill states that said John and David Woods res in Pa/John Archer, and John W. Stump, exec of John Stump, vs Rebecca Nowland, Maria Nowland, Edward Nowland, Sophia Nowland, William Fulton, and Matilda his wife and Edward Benedict Stark, heirs and representatives of Peregrine Nowland, decd; bill states that Peregrine Nowland, late of Har Co, decd, was in his lifetime largely indebted to John Stump of said co, also now decd; and that said Peregrine Nowland died indebted in or about 1820, leaving a widow Rebecca Nowland who became his administratrix and the following chilrden and heirs: Eliza, Maria, Edward, Sophia, and Matilda. Eliz married a certain ___ Stark, and is since dead, leaving one child Edward Benedict; Matilda married a certain William Fulton, all of whom res out of the state. Said Peregrine Nowland died seized of certain real est in town of Bush, consisting of a Tavern House and lot adj - S. Archer, T. Kell/I. D. Maulsby and John H. Price, Harf Co, have associated themselves as partners in the practice of law

151. ICP Sep 10 1829/Winston D. Smith candidate for Gen Assembly/Sale decreed by Equity Court of Harf Co in case of Jacob Michael vs Harriet Osborn/Sale of farm where he res on Broad Creek, about 700 a., new stone grist mill, covered with slate, a saw mill, store hosue, new farm barn, stables; on the prop is the old "Enterprize Furnace, "which belongd to the Valentine's- Nathan Bemis, on the premises

152. ICP Sep 17 1829/Died about 2 o'clock 8 inst, Hugh Dever aged about 80, native of Ireland, but for the last 58 yrs, a res of this co/Trustee's sale farm whereof John Hanson, late of Harf Co, died seized, consisting of two tracts, Drew's Enlargment and Rumney Marsh, about 200 a.; also had a herring fishery - Albert Constable, trustee/Sale at his res nr Hall's Cross Road of wagon and harness, 4 hd of horses, 4 hd of cattle, 14 hd of sheep, 1 Dearborne wagon, furniture, 42 a. of land and other items - James Stillings

153. ICP Sep 24 1829/No new items

154. ICP Oct 1 1829/Opposition article to Dr. George E. Mitchell/Notice is given to George St. Clair, Mary St. Clair, Alizanna St. Clair, Martha St. Clair, Ann St. Clair, William St. Clair, James St. Clair, heirs of Lester St. Clair, late of Harf Co, decd, that the subscribers have been appointed as commissioners on the petition of Hannah Clark, to make partition or valuation of the lands whereof the said Lester St. Clair died seized, being parts of two tracts called St. Clair's Good Luck and Clackstone's Forrest - Abel Alderson, James Nelson, William Careins, Commissioners/New Bridge Hotel Oyster Cellar, occ by James Gaskins - James M. Miller, John M. Cooper, Balt

155. ICP Oct 8 1829/Dissolution of associaton of I. D. Maulsby and Jno. H. Price /John Y. Day, nr King's Tavern, will rent farm between Great Falls of Gunpowder and Bird River known as Taylor's Mount

156. ICP Oct 15 1829/Benjamin Silver offers reward for two fat cattle which strayed from a drove on Thurs betwen Bel-Air and the Little Falls Bridge /Albert Constable and Susan Wilson adm of William Wilson, Harf Co, decd, to sell his pers est/James Billingslea adm of Jervis Gilbert, Harf Co, decd

157. ICP Oct 22 1829/Married Tues evening last by Rev Wm. Stephenson, Doctor Wakeman B. Hopkins, to Miss Hannah R. Worthington, all of this Co/Married Thurs last by Rev Wm. Finney, George Moore, to Miss Elizabeth Gilbert, all of this co/Married Mon last by same, Jacob J. Mohlen, of Balt, to Miss Mary Ann Mitchell, of this co/Died Fri last at his res, after a long and painful illness, John Norris, one of the Associate Judges of the Orphans'Court of this Co/Francis J. Dallam vs John W. Carlisle in Harf Co Court of Equity

158. ICP Oct 29 1829/Wiliam F. Miller insolvent debtor of Harf Co - Samuel Bradford, trustee

159. ICP Nov 5 1829/Samuel Bradford appointed Associate Judge of the Orphans' Court of this co vice John Norris, decd/Married Thurs evening last by Rev Park, Miss Jane Heaps, to William Demoss, both of this co/Died at New Orleans 24 Sep of prevailing fever, William D. Jolly, formerly of Harf Co, in 28th yr of his age; he had established himself in New Orleans as a merchant - Balt. Chron./Bible distribution - Robert H. Archer, chairman of executive

committee/William Miller tanner and currier to continue to carry business at the old stand lately occ by his decd father, Jacob Miller for 40 yrs past, in Front st, Old Town, direct opp Bull's Head Tavern, Balt/Constables's sale of right of Luther A. Norris to land in Bush River Neck, negro men named Lewis, and Parker, at suit of Jacob A. Preston - Hugh McCown, Constable/Improved plough - John McKenney, Jr

160. ICP Nov 12 1829/Death of Revolutionary soldier, at his res in Kent Co, Brigadier General Philip Reed, at a very advanced age - Telegraph/Notice is given to Penelia Kidd, widow of James Kidd decd; James Ward and Rachel his wife; Henry Scarff & James Scarff, Joshua Scarff and Julia Ann Scarff, children of the aforementioned Henry Scarff; Elizabeth Shaw, James Tarman and Rhoda his wife, James Kidd and Joshua Kidd, heirs at law of said James Kidd, late of Harf Co, decd on petition of Moses St. Clair to make partitiion or valuation of the lands whereof said James Kidd died seized, being tract called Kidd's Troubles - John W. Rutledge, James Nelson, Samuel Reed, Commnrs

161. ICP Nov 19 1829/Married some time since in Ohio, Richard C. Langdon, Editor of The Farmer's Record and Xenia Gazette, to Miss Abarilla Mitchell, dau of Edward Mitchell of this Co/Married Tues evening 10 inst by Rev M. L. Fullerton, James Johnson, M. D., formerly of this Co, to Miss Jane, 2nd dau of Joseph Gabby of Frederick Co, Md/Sale by order of Orphans' Court of Harf Co: household furniture at the late dwelling of John Norris - Isaac Tyson, exec; farm is for rent; apply to Mary Norris, on the premises/Orphans' Court sale at former res of late Freeborn Brown of part of pers est of Mary B. Brown decd, including several slaves - Samuel Bradford, adm/Sheriff's sale of right of John Blake to two tracts: Bilberry Hall and Ewing's Contrivance, the purch of Thomas A. Hays and Otho Scott, at suit of Thomas A. Hays and Otho Scott - John Kean, Sheriff/Sale of right of William Baxtor to tract called Bond's pleasant Hills, 20 a., and furniture at suit of John B. Ford's admrs /Thomas A. Hays and Stevenson Archer adm of Archer Hays, Harf Co, decd/Samuel Bradford adm of Mary B. Brown

162. ICP Nov 26 1829/Sale of pers est of William Gladden, decd - Jacob Gladden Jr, exec/James Hughes, insolvent debtor of Harf Co, discharged from imprisonment

163. ICP Dec 3 1829/Case of Sheriff Swearingen - born Jan 29 1800 in Frederick Co, Va; his ancestors were on both side wealthy and respectable; admitted to the bar in Virginia and Indiana, and also in Alleghany Co, Md; in 1823 appointed a captain of a militia company and elected sheriff of Washington Co in Oct 1827; married 12 Feb 1824 Mary Scott, a young lady who had been sent by her parents res in Cumberland to the school of Miss Inglis in Hagerstown, and who had just completed her course of education in that seminary. Miss Scott was before allied to Swearingen by ties of consanguinity, and her parents being wealthy, he obtained by this marriage a considerable accession to his fortune. He avers however that his motives in marrying her were not sordid, and that their harmony was uninterrupted for more than a year - nor did any material cause of dissatisfaction occur until the summer of 1827. Swearingen has been accused of two attempts to destroy the life of his wife before the actual murder - one by upsetting a gig over a precipice, on the Alleghany mountain, himself leaping out on the bank; another by taking her on horse back over the Potomac at a dangerous fording. Both of these imputed attempts he solemnly denies. His fatal attachment to the notorious Rachel

Cuningham took place in the summer of 1827. Her he from this time maintained at his own expense, shifting her from house to house, and from neighborhood to neighborhood, to avoid the indignation of the populace, which persued her wherever her character was known. ...He and his wife were return- ing from a camp-meeting which had been held in the vicinity of Cumberland. After leaving Cresap-town on Monday the 8th of Septemeber 1828, they had occasion to pass a farm belonging to Swearingen, and occupied by a tenant. At this farm his wife desired to call, but he, knowing that Rachel Cunningham was there, oppposed the wish of wife. This opposition on his part caused her to suspect that this paramour was on the farm, and increased her anxiety to call. He however still refused..."I became very angry, and as my horse was a little in the rear of hers, I pushed him on, let the rein go, and with my right fist, and with all my force, I stuck her on the back part of her head, just behind the ear, and knocked her off her horse."..The blow proved distinctly fatal - he immediately alighted, and found his wife dead ... Perceiving from the former suspicions of a design to murder her - from the immediate vicinity of Rachel Cunnihgham...he took up the corpse in order to convey it to a place where the roughness of the ground might render it more probable that death had been occasioned by the mere fall from her horse...The Coroner's jury returned that she came to her death by and act of Providence," and on Tuesday the body was interred in the family burying ground adj Cumber- land. Suspicion however becoming stronger, it was disinterred on Thurs; alarmed he fled, accompanied by Rachel Cunningham; he was apprehended at New Orleans in Feb 1829, tried in Alleghany Co court and executed at Cumberland on 2 Oct, having not yet attained the age of thirty

164. ICP Dec 3 1829/Married Tues evening last by Rev Wm. Stephenson, John H. Price of this place, to Miss Grace Williams, dau of James Williams, of Stafford, all of this co/Married 27 ult by Rev W. Finney, Captain Arthur Woolford, to Miss Abigail Williams, all of this co/Geo. Wm. Hall, Constant Friendship, Harf Co, seeks to hire farm hands/George Griffith seeks to hire young healthy negro woman/Stray steer - Wm. Silver/John O. Bageley, Deer Creek, nr Darlington, reports a stray steer/Farm for sale in pursuance of general order of Balt Co Court in relation to insolvent debtors, trustee of Isaac T. Willson, will sell tract called Bell Tavern, lately in the posses- sion of said Wilson, binding upon Bush River in Harf Co; see George Bradford adj the land or J. D. Learned, trustee, Balt/Sale by decree of High Court of Chancery of farm in Bush River Neck called Rumney, 360 a.; also land called Sheppard's Good Friendship, 35 a., farm is former res of Edward Hall, decd /James Paul adm of Thomas Paul, Har Fo, decd/Samuel Henry, Lloyd, and Josiah Mathews, insolvent debtors of Harf Co, to be disch from imprisonment

165. ICP Dec 10 1829/By order of orphans' court of Harf Co, sale at late res of Jacob Baxter, decd, horses, cows, sheep, hogs, yoke of oxen, ox cart, dearborn wagon, corn, rye, oats, potatoes, cider and casks, cider mills, copper still, 60 gallons, farming utensils, furniture - Samuel Baxter, adm /Sheriff's sale in Abingdon right of John Saunders to tract called Thompson's Fortune and tract Williams' Fortune; also tract called Jones Inheritance - John Kean, sheriff/Constable's sale in Bush River Neck of right of Luther A. Norris to negro man named Ned, negro woman named Grace and female child named Lucy 16 months old/Constable's sale at Michaelsville of negro man named Frederick, prop of Henry Christie and Stephen Frisby (men of colour) at suit of Joseph Brownley/Sale of house which he now occupies in Bel-Air at main st and Port Deposit road - Abraham Jarrett, Jr/Farm for sale where he res in Harf

Co, 170 a., Jehu Smith/Commissioners of the School fund will meet - Thomas Hope/John Donn and Joshua Whitaker, insolvent debtors, to be disch from imprisonment

166. ICP Dec 17 1829/Married Tues last by Rev Richardson, John H. Munnikhuysen, to Miss Priscilla Ann Bond, dau of Z.O. Bond, all of this co /Pocket book lost between Balt and Turner's tavern - Henry Dorsey of Edward at Belle-Air /Sheriff's sale of right of Edward Kerr to tract, Abrahams Inheritance, at suit of James Stephenson and sale of right of Edward Kerr to farm whereon said Kerr lives, at the suit of Robert Taylor

167. ICP Dec 24 1829/Married Tues evening last by Rev Wm. Finney, Albert Constable of this place, to Miss Hannah S., eld dau of Dr. John Archer, of Rock Run, all of this co/Married on 10 inst by same,. Aquila Wiles, to Miss Mary Bayless, all of this co/Died at his res in this co 13 inst, Samuel Harper Senr. aged 74/Rev Reed agent of the Tract society to preach in Bel-Air /John Chauncey adm of Cornelius Cole/John Evatt senr, trustee to sell house and 12 a. of land, late the prop and res of James Beatty, decd, in town of Dublin, Harf Co/Sheriff's sale of right of George M. Wheeler to tracts, Brotherly Care and Pearson's Range, conveyed by James B. Wheeler to said George M. Wheeler and Rebecca Wheeler/James McCrodan has returned again to Harford and opened an English and Mathematical Academy nr Hickory Tavern

168. ICP Dec 31 1829/Died at his res in this co Sat evening last, Alexander Hanna, at a very advanced age/To be sold at the house of Mortimore Cunningham, in Abingdon, house and lot seized and taken as prop of Theodore Delmas, to satisfy a judgment due Samuel M. Richardson - Jas. Cochran, Col/Sheriff's sale of right of William Temple to land of 20 a. adj land which the double run passes, purch by said Temple of Thomas Ayres; also 2 a. with stone house, at suit of Thomas Ayres/Commissioners appointed by Cecil Co Court to partition and value real est of Jeremiah Baker, decd - Henry Chamberlaine, Wm. W. Ramsay, L. H. Evans, John N. Black, James Campbell

169. ICP Jan 7 1830/William H. Fasquet offers for sale a farm in Cecil Co, on Bohemia River, 236 1/4 a./Letters remaining at P.O. Bel Air: Mrs. Elizabeth Brown; Mrs. Elizabeth Barnett; Benjamin H. Baxter; John Bond; Mrs. Elizabeth Cain; John Clendinen; Jacob Cline; Elizabeth Denbow; Jennette Duvall; Rev Reuben H. Davis; John Y. Day; John Daugherty; Mrs. Teresa Edwards; Isaac J. Ely; Mrs. Rebecca Fish; Miss Sophia Fullerton; John Forward; Rev Charles T. Ford; Robert Fish; William Forwood; John Forwood; Gilbert Funk; Abraham Garrett; Robert Glenn; Mr. Garrett; Abraham Gibson; Miss Cassandra Green; Thomas A. Hays; David Harry; John D. Harris; James Huggins; Asael Hichcock; Joseph Harlan; William Holland; Aaron Holland; Henry H. Johns; Dr. Caleb M. Johnson; John Kean; Joseph Kenedy; Mount Ararat Lodge; James Lytle, jr; Miss Minerva Monk; Miss Mary A. Mason; John Magness; George McGlaughlin; James McCrodan; Miss Rebecca Newlin; David Newlin; Alexander Norris; David Norris; Robert Parker, jr; James Pannell; D. H. Preston; Mrs. E. Raphel; William Rutledge; John Rogers; Vincent Richardson; Miss Belinda Slade; Charles S. Sewell; John Scaff; Samuell Sutton; Thos. Street of Thos.; Otho Scott; Samuel Smith; Silas Silver; William Smithson; Robert W. Smith; John Thompson of Thomas, sr; Elysha Tayson; James Tredwell; Thomas Tredway; Mrs. Lydia Wodsworth; Archibald Wilson; Isaac T. Wilson; Daniel Wa...; Nathan Walton; Jonathan Warner - John Robinson, P.M/High Court of Chancery sale of tracts, Common Garden, 55 a.; Briary Island, 22 a.; and pt of Sheppard's Good

Friendship, in Bush River Neck, of which William Osborn, late of Harf Co, decd, died seized/Sheriff's sale of negro boy, 8-day clock, furniture, goods and chattels of Sarah James adm of Sedgwick James, at suit of John Archer and John W. Stump/Report of stray mare by James W. Mitchell of Balt

170. ICP Jan 14 1830/Died Mon morning 4 inst at his res in this co, James Hope, in 58th yr/Died Wed 6v Jan inst at res of his father in this village, James Taylor of Wm. in 47th yr; thus have two aged and infirm parents been stript of their only staff and solace, a good son and brother/Died 8 Dec last at Fort Adams, Mississippi, William Monks, in 42nd yr; he was born in Abingdon, Harf Co, where he res until 1817, when he removed to Fort Adams where he has since been actively engaged in the mercantile business; he left a wife and three children/Samuel Bradford, auditor, requests that creditors of Robert Saunders, Harf Co, decd, present their claims/Sheriff's sale at suit of Abraham Jarrett, of title of Henry M'Atee to tract called Belle Farm, Mine Bank, Partnership Dissolved, and Turkey Range, and negro Milly aged 25 /Committed to my custody, a negro man by name of Stephen Bishop; about 45, 5 ft 7-8 inch; says he is prop of Elias Warthon, of Fairfax Co, Va - John Kean, Sheriff of Harf Co

171. ICP Jan 21 1830/Married Sun morning 10 inst by Rev Thomas McGee, Benedict Hanson, to Miss Lydia Barnes, all of this co/married Thurs 14 inst by Rev Morrison, William Cairns to Miss Elizabeth Vance, all of this co /Abingdon Academy will by open to receive pupils - Charles S. Sewall, Pres of the board of Trustees; John C. Norris, clerk/Sale of prop: house in Bel-Air, at present occ by Miss Nancy Bond; 150 a. nr Deer Creek, being farm on which Morgan Richardson lately res; tract of 30 a. called The Falling Branch; lot being pt of real est of late Joseph Wheeler nr Hickory Tavern with dwelling occ by John Judd - Wm. Richardson, Bel-Air/Sheriff's sale of right of Ephraim G. Gover, Elizabeth Gover, Robert Gover, Jarrett Gover, Margaretta Gover, Philip R. Gover, Samuel W. Lee, Mary Lee and Priscilla Wilson to tract called Rupalta, 20 a., at suit of Daniel M. Cooley/Sheriff's sale of pers prop of Thomas Ayres, at the suit of Samuel Bradford/Albert Constable will attend at his office in Belk-Air on Mon and Tues each week/Sale of farm in Harf Co about 1 mile from Little Falls of Gunpowder - Col. Edward A. Howard, within 3 miles of the place

172. ICP Jan 28 1830/Loss of the Hornet; her Commander was our friend and neighbour. Capt. Norris was born and educated nr this village. ...He was a husband and a father and we sincerely hope that his country will do all in its power to alleviate the calamity which has befallen those, who were dependent upon him for protection and support. In addition to her Commander, we number among those of our acquaintance, on board of the Hornet, a son of Charles S. Sewell, of Abingdon, and Thomas B. Harrison, of Baltimore, the latter a schoolmate of our earlier years; (the Hornet foundered and sank with the loss of all on board when an unusually severe gale came on, driving her from her moorings to put to sea off Tampico, Mexico)/Church and Masonic Hall in Bel-Air nearly finished - I. D. Maulsby, Chas. S. Sewell, Thomas Hope, Building Committee/Married Tues evening 26 ult by Rev Poteet, Peter Streigthoof to Miss Elizabeth Baker, all of this co/Married Thurs evening last, by Jacob Job, Jehu Montgomery of Harf Co, to Miss Catharine McCullough of Cecil Co/Constable's sale of right of Cadwalader Jones to tract on which he res to satisfy a judgment due Isaac Hawkins - John S. Ward, Constable

173. ICP Feb 4 1830/Married Thurs evening by Rev Parke, Benjamin Brooks, to Miss Elizabeth Barnett, both of this co/Married same day by same, John Ford to Miss Martha Darraugh, both of this co/Married Mon evening 25 ult by Rev McGee, Edward Stansbury, to Miss Corelia Howard, both of Balt co/Died Thurs morning last, Mrs. Rebecca Blackston, relict of John Blackston, of this co /Sarah Bull adm of Walter Bull/Sheriff's sale of right of James Duncan to tract, Saulsbury Plains, 324 a.; sale of right of tract called Addition to Ward's Intent, 71 a. and tract McCleery's Half Purchase, 53 a. and a negro man, prop of Roger Street, at suit of State of Md, use of William Careins/ sale of title of Abraham Baker to tract, Orr's Survey, 144 a., at suit of above; sale of 135 and horses of Joshua M. Amos/Testimonials to the effectiveness of Judkins' Ointment, includes letter form Danl. M. Cunningham, Harf Co, who received relief from rhumatism after using the ointment

174. ICP Feb 11 1830/Sale on the premises, Broad Creek, where subscriber res, of horses, cows, hogs, farming utensils, furniture - John Harmer/Sale at late res of John Watters, decd, nr Coopstown, pers est of said decd - Esther Watters, adm

175. ICP Feb 18 1830/Married Tues 9 inst by Rev O'Brien, John Shipley, of Balt Co, to Miss Ann Doran, of this co/Married Thurs last by Rev Ewing of Pa, Lewis King, to Miss Jane Heaps, both of this co/Died very suddenly of gout in the stomach at Jericho, seat of late Parker Hall Lee, in this co, Sun 14 Feb inst, Samuel Worthington Lee, in 59th yr of his age (long obit)/Died Sun last at his father's res in this co, William Prigg, aged 24/Sale of tract late the prop of William Baxter, senr., at suit of Joseph Sanders, adm of Margaret - James Cochran, Constable/Wanted - a single man to manage Mount Friendship Farm with a few hands ; enquire of Abraham Jarrett, on the farm, or of A. L. Jarrett, in Bel-Air, at Stephen Jones - A. L. Jarrett, Amanda C. Jarrett, Mount Friendship/Sale by order of Orphans' Court pers est of Benedict Stewart of negro girl aged 17 to serve til she is 31, three negro boys, slaves for life, one 14, one 12, and the other 7, cows and furniture - James McGaw, adm/Sheriff's sale of right of Robert Gover, to tract called Rupalta, 200 a., at suit of Thomas A. hays adm of Gilbert Jones

176. ICP Feb 25 1830/Married at res of Geo. R. Amoss, by Rev Keech, Thurs evening last Daniel Raymond of Balt city to Miss Sarah E. Amoss, 2nd dau of Isaac R. Amoss, late of Balt Co/Married Thurs 11 inst by Rev O'Brien, Joseph Devoe, to Miss Clara Green, all of this co/Married Thurs evening last by Rev Park, Alexander McComas, Jr. to Miss Mary Streett, all of this co/Married Thurs 18 inst at Friends Meeting House, Saratoga steet Balt, Doctor Thomas Worthington, of Harf Co, to Elizabeth Gillingham, of that city/Sunday school Fair in Abingdon - M. T. Bond, Sec.; donations may be left at Mrs. H. Simmons'/Trustees' sale of real est of George Macatee, decd, of a farm of 287 a., of two tracts, Isaac's Enlargment and Hard Bargain, on Deer Creek - Henry Macatee, Samuel Macatee, trustees/117 a. of land for sale - Bennet Love/Saml. Forwood will sell at his res horses, cattle, sheep, hogs, oxen, farming utensils

177. ICP Mar 4 1830/Married at Fawn Grove, Pa, on Mon 21 ult by Rev Ewing, Edward J. Markland, to Miss Frances C. McJilton, both of Darlington in this co /Married Tues evening 23 ult by Rev Slicer, Joshua C. Fuller to Miss Frances Hall, both of Balt Co/Married Sun evening last by Rev Richardson, John F.

Madden to Miss Ann Elizabeth Sneed/Appointments for Harf Co: Justices of the Peace: James Steel; William Allen; George Bradford; William Smith of Samuel; William Glenn; Hosier Barnes; Walter T. Hall; Stephen Watters; James McGaw; John Donn; Stephen Jones; Robert Richardson; Platt Whitaker; George H. Wilson; Edward M. Guyton; James S. M'Comas; Amos Watters; James Lytle; Vincent Norris; Hanson Courtney; Edward Rutledge; Samuel Brown; Jas. Wilson (Mine Branch); Robt. S. Henderson; John W. Rutledge; Thomas G. Howard; John Hopkins; Samuel Reed; Joseph Davis; Jacob Hoopman; David Silver; Thomas Courtney; Benjamin Richardson; Benjamn Pitcock; James Alexander; William Price; William Lindsay; Harry D. Gough; Joseph Worthington; Edward Prigg of William; Edward F. Bussey; Joseph Robinson; Thomas C. Stump; Charles Gilbert; Samuel Whitaker; Benjamin Painer of Benjamin; Corbin Poteet; David Lee Malsby; William Magness, sr; John Hannah; Rowland Rodgers; Thomas Smithson, of Nathaniel; Zacheus O. Bond; Samuel Smith; John Smith; Richard Coale; Wm Wilson (miller); Dr. John Sappington; Henry McAtee; Peter V. Morrison; Hamilton Morgan; Thomas Street of John; Thomas Hannaway; Joshua Amos of Robert; Alexander Amos; Isaac Stansbury; James Duncan; John Heaton; William G. Dove; John Anderson; Luther Jarrett; Thomas Fleaharty; James Tredwell; Everett S. Hughes; William Brooks; Robert McCausland; Daniel Bay; Nathan S. Bemis; Samuel Bradford; John C. Forwood; James Gover; John Lewis; John C. Norris; Thos. M. Ricketts; Francis Delmas; Robt. W. Holland; John A. Amos; Basil Grafton; Timothy Keen; John Smithson; Jacob Michael; Robert Parker; Richard Ashton; Thomas Foard; Amos Osborne; John Heaps; Edward Norris of Edward; Danl. Cunningham; Matthew Hawkins; Charlton M. Waltham; Ananias Divers; John Wilson nr Nelson's Mill; Thomas Bay; Henry P. Ruff; Richard D. Lee; John Kirk; Henry G. Watters; Dr. Archibald Dorsey - Orphans Court: John Forwood, John Streett, James Pannel - Surveyor: John Love/Sale of farm on which Joseph Kennedy formerly lived, 106 a. - John Kean/Land for sale - on Deer Creek - Eli Smith/Chancery sale of mortgaged est of Thomas Kelly by trustee, John Forwood/R. H. Davis, Bel-Air, wants to hire man servant

178. ICP Mar 11 1830/Married Thurs evening 2d inst by Rev Parke, Samuel Richardson, to Miss Priscilla Worthington, both of Darlington, in this co/Died Fri morning 26 ult at his res in the co, Henry Fullard, aged about 83/Plantation for sale about 3 miles west of Bel-Air adj Jonathan Warner, 300-400 a.; enquire of Rebecca R. Yellott nr the Great Falls of Gunpowder, Balt Co/Constable's sale at suit of Peter Hopman and Jacob Hopman, right of Aquila Carrol to tracts, Gravely Hills, Woods Close, Cook's Rest and Royal Exchange and two cows

179. ICP Mar 18 1830/James Wallace candidate for sheriff/Married Thurs 6 inst by Rev Dr. Martin, Robert Cowan, to Miss Elizabeth Kerr, all of Lower Chanceford, York Co, Pa/Married same day by Rev Poteet, James Logue, to Miss Elizabeth Amos, both of this co/Married same day by Rev Poisal, Luther M. Jarrett to Miss Julia Ann Scarff, both of this co/Married Tues 9th, by Rev Parke, Elisha Davis to Miss Mary James, both of the co/Married Thurs evening last, by Rev Herrin, Joseph B. Chaftin to Miss Ruth Pariot, all of Balt Co/Sale by John Forwood on the farm where late Clement Green lived and died, mare, oxen, cows, ewes and lambs, negro girl about 10, and furniture/For rent - dweling in town of Bush, known by name of the White House, at present occ by Henry Smith; apply to A. J. Thomas, Havre-de-Grace/William Lester gives notice that his wife Mary Lester, having left his bed and board he will pay not debts by her contracted

180. ICP Mar 25 1830/Married Thurs 25 ult by Rev John R. Keech, William Thompson, to Miss Mary Jones, dau of late Daniel Jones, all of Harf Co/Died Mon 15 inst, William M. infant son of John L. Johnson, of this co/Died Tues 16 inst, Rev John Allen, Professor of Mathematicks in Univ of Md, in 70th yr/Sale of horses, sheep, hogs, 2 yokes of oxen, ox cart, light market wagon, ploughs, harrows and farming utensils generally; also his farm is for rent - Caleb Pue/Late Sheriff's sale - at suit of Lydia Barnes, negro woman named Eliza aged 28 and child, late the prop of John Donn - H. H. Jonn's, late sheriff/Tanner's bark bought - Joshua and John Husband/Stray cow came to the subscribers, res at the Upper Cross Roads, Harf Co - James M'Claskey

181. ICP Apr 1 1830/Married Tues 23 by Rev Park, James Singleton to Miss Martha Ann Clark, both of this co/Dr. R. N. Allen has removed to his former res on Deer Creek/Doctr. Munnikhuysen has located in Bel-Air/Nancy Bond, Bel-Air, intending to remove to Balt, will sell furniture/Mercer potatoes for sale - John M'Kenney, Jr/Smithville Woollen Cloth Factory, on Winters Run, 3 miles from Bel-Air - rented by Tilghman, Fish & Co, to conduct the Woollen business/Constable's sale at suit of John Anderson and Elizabeth Bell, adm of Robert Bell, at Frances Smith's Tavern, right of Joseph K. Hopkins, to tracts, Lion Tents or Neighbours' Good Will - John Carsins, constable/Horse Virginian will stand - Richard D. Lee

182. ICP Apr 8 1830/Cecil Mills, nr Port Deposit Bridge, in Cecil Co, prop of James Bosley, of Balt, were consumed by fire on Fri evening last, together with a large building designed for a tavern; these mills were nearly new and constructed in the best manner and the flour manufactured there had obtained a high character in foreign markets; buildings were insured to the amount of $35,000 which will not cover the loss estimated at perhaps $50,000/John Riddle was tried at our last Court as an accomplice of Wilson and Poteet, who shot at Mr. Disney, one of the Keepers of the Penitentiary, and condemned to ten years imprisonment in that institution. He was removed from our jail a few days since to his lodgings; but it appears he did not like his quarters, as he broke through the ceiling of the room in which he was confined, made his way to the garret, thence through the scuttle, and descending by the lightning rod made his escape/Abingdon Fair projected by some of the young ladies of that town to assist them in the promotion and encouragement of a Sunday School has for some weeks past sedulously engaged all the fairy fingers of the village and its vicinity. The result has far surpassed expectation. The Fair was held in the new Academy lately erected in Abingdon, which was tastefully decorated for the occasion. The tables were spread with every description of "Fancy's fairy frostwork."/Died Sat last at his res on Long Green, Rev Joseph Slee, of the Meth Episc Church, in 51st yr/Died Mon morning last, Mrs. Ann relict of Aquila Hall of Long Green, at an advanced age/A Card of thanks from The Young Ladies attached to the Abingdon Sunday School for articles for their Fair - Sophia Fullerton, Sec'ry/Election of Five Directors of Havre-de-Grace Ferry company - George Bartol, Treasurer /Sale at his res nr Darlington, of horses, farming utensils, cows, sheep, Hogs - John Brannan/Sheriff's sale right of Abner Gilbert whereon said Gilbert now lives, 90 a./Sale of farm lying on Thomas' Run, Harf Co, 190 a., includes saw mill - John Slee/Sale of tract on Deer Creek called William's Discovery, late prop of Nathan S. Bemis - A. W. Bradford, trustee; includes two-story log dwelling, stable, cooper's shop, about 3/4 mile form ore bank belonging to Evan T. Elicott

183. Letters remaining at P.O. Bel-Air: Stevenson Archer; Thos. Ayres; John Archer Amoss; John Blaney; James Baker; Mrs. Eliza. Bussey; Dr. Henry G. Boyer; John E. Bull; Mrs. Sarah Bull; John Bleake; George W. Bradford; Miss Eliza Calwel; Charles McAnn; William Coale; John Chauncey; Miss Sarah E.Clendinen; Dr. Archibald Dorsey; Martin Denbow; Miss Susan R. Dallam; Thomas Dorney; John Donaher; William M. Elliott; William Everitt; William Forewood; Rheubin Forewood; Morice Foaly; Rev Wm Finney; Gustavus Frank; Jacob Gladden Jr; Abraham Gybson; Crawford Gorrel; James Guyton; John M. Green; George Henderson; Abraham Harmer; Richard Hooper; James N. Henderson; James Hervey; John Huff; Aaron Harkins; Richd. F. Hollis; Mrs. Mary Harry; Henry H. Johns; A. C. Johnson; Benj G. Jones; Thos. Johnson; Charles Johnson; Mrs. Margarett Johnson; C. D. W. Johnson; Theophilus Jones; Miss Susan Ann Johnson of Thos.; Matthew Kennard; The Worshipful Master of Mount Ararat Lodge; Mrs. Aberilla M. Langdon; Mrs. Elizabeth Lewis; Mrs. Elizabeth B. La Rue; Abraham Mulligeur; George McCullough; David J. Maulsby; William Michael; John B. McFaddon; Amos Mccomas; Job Mitton; Samuel McGay; James Mead; Silvester McAtee; Miss Ann M. Marshall; Mrs. Mary Martin; James McConnell; John McComass; Mrs. Sarah McCracken; Stewart Marshall; John A. Mitchell; Samuel Moody; Joseph Moore; Andrew Miller; Henry G. Maynadier; Isaac Norris; D. Norris; David Pyle; George Pereman; Mrs. Ann Peryman; Mrs. Eliza Ann Preston; Scott Preston; William Pyle; Robert Richardson; Thomas Reed; George Rister; Vincent Richardson Isaac Robinson; Miss Henriettta Richardson; Samuel Smith; Jarad Sappington; James Smith; Zacary Stroble; Roger Street; Otho Scott; Thomas Sappington; John Tredway; Joseph Turner; Edward Tredway; Miss Rebecca Tucker; William Temple; Elizabeth S. Trimble; Rachael Tredway; Joseph Ward; Thos Whitehead; John Ward; Andrew Wilson; Chris. Wilson; Nathan Walton; Henry Webster; John Woodland - John Robinson, Postmaster/Dr. W. B. Hopkins, associate of Dr. R. H. Archer, in the practice of medicine, has removed to the house adj store of Messrs T. A. & N. Hays, Bel-Air/It appears to the Harf Co Court that Henry Cooper, Philip Cooper, Nathaniel Cooper, Basil Cooper, Francis Cooper, Elizabeth Cooper and Mary Cooper are persons entitled to elect to take the lands mentioned in the petition of Ann Lennen for the division of real est of Henry Cooper, decd; notice is hereby given

184. ICP Apr 15 1830/All but half a sheet of this issue is missing/No new item in the fragment remaining

185. ICP Apr 22 1830/The horse, Young Brilliant, will stand at Col. Jacob Michael's Store, Daniel Michael's and at subscriber's stable - Wm. Michael /Sale of pers est of Alexander Hanna, decd - John Hanna, adm/In consequence of having declined farming, will sell horses, cows, sheep, hogs, wagon, a cariole, furniture, ploughs, harrows, harness - Bennet Love/Wm. H. Pasquet will sell a farm in Cecil Co, on Bohemia River/Tavern for sale at Bush; also dwelling house and blacksmith's shop; apply to David Maulsby, nr Gover's Mill on Deer Creek/John Curry, Junr insolvent debtor, to be disch from imprisonment/Richard Webster adm of Woolsey, Harf Co/Joshua Rutledge will stand his horse, Sir Henry, at various places/John Jervis will stand Young Bacchus /Proposals will be rec'd for prupose of building two fireproof offices in Bel-Air - John Forwood, Thomas A. Hays, John Street, William Nelson, James Pannell, Samuel Bradford, Commissioners

186. ICP Apr 29 1830/Married Thurs evening last at Franklinvile, Balt Co, by Rev Herring, John T. Sneed to Miss Lydia Mitchell, dau of Edward Mitchell of

this co/For rent - store house in Bel-Air, now occ by Messrs. Munnikhuysen and Gover - Jason Moore/Trustee's sale of Tavern stand, in town of Bush, whereof Peregrine Nowland late of Harf Co died seized, at present occ by Aquila Knight - A. Bradford, Trustee

187. ICP May 6 1830/Married in Balt Thurs evening last by Rev Breckenridge, George M. Gill, to Miss Ann, dau of late Thos. McElderry/Abingdon Academy has engaged James Steen, A. M. of Balt - Charles S. Sewell, Pres of Bd of Trustees/Land for sale in Deer Creek, res of William Ely, decd, farm of about 115 a., Jacob Ely, William Ely/Trustee's sale of res of James Beatty, decd, in town of Dublin - John Evatt, Sr, trustee/Equity case - Duncan & others vs William R. Presbury and others, heirs of George Presbury, of Wm./Blacksmith wanted - Joseph Harlan/Regimental Court Martial, 40th Regt, is hereby detailed, to consist of Capt Thomas Hope, Pres, Capt John Archer Amos, Capt Thos. Gassaway Howard, Lieut John S. Sterrett, Lieut. James B. Amos, Lieut John Thompson, Major Wm. Richardson, Judge Advocate; to be convened at house of James McClasky (Upper Cross Roads) Fri 18 Jun next - I. D. Maulsby, Colonel/Commissioners of Harf Co appoint Amos Waters, Keeper of the Standard of Weights and Measures/Sheriff's sale right of Kent Mitchell to tract called Contrivance, at suit of William Sappington/Sheriff's sale of est of George M. Wheeler: tract, Brotherly Care and tract called Pearson's Range, at suit of Jacob Hoover

188. ICP May 13 1830/Henry Whittemore, John W. Green, Bennet M. Bilingslea, Harf Co, to be discharged from imprisonment

189. ICP Jun 24 1830/Thomas Hope exec of James Hope/W. Ashdown continues to carry on the business of wool carding, spinning & fulling at the Factory of Thos. A. Hays on Winter's Run/Woollen Manufactory- John Lilly has taken the factory belonging to Jacob Gladden Jr nr Rocks of Deer Creek/Wool carding - Jacob Hoopman is now fixing his carding machine at his mill in Harf Co, 1 mile from Frances Smith's Stone Tavern and expects to be able to card wool by first of June next/Drs. R. N. Allen aand Bennett F. Bussey had formed a partnership for the purpose of jointly pursuing the practice of medicine/William Barnes insolvent debtor to be disch from imprisonment/Edward Mitchell being desirious of closing his affairs in this place with a view of going to the Westward, has appointed Richard C. Langdon his agent for that purpose/Dr. C. H. Bradford has comenced practice of medicine in Bel-Air; he res with his father, Samuel Bradford and occ office adj/Sale of farm, mill - Edward Mitchell/Sale of farm called Spring Forest, 200 a., adj lands of Benjamin Silver, Zephaniah Bayless, Robert Hawkins, Joshua Husband; enquire of Geo. H. Wilson res nr premises or to subscriber, John Wilson of Wm/Farm for sale on Long Green, Balt Co adj Moses Jenkins - Isaac Ford on the premises

190. ICP Jun 24 1830/Joseph Brown vs Robert McLaughlin, Frances McLaughlin, Samuel McLaughlin, George McLaughlin, John McLaughlin and Nancy McLaughlin; the bill in this case states that Samuel Smith, late of Harf Co decd, devised parcel of land in said co called Stoney Ridge and Paca's(?) Enlargement, 221 a., to his children: William Smith, George Smith, David Smith, Margaret Deaver, Jane Smith and Ann McLaughlin, in fee simple; that the said devisees, after laying off 37 1/2 a. of said land to the said Margaret Deaver, as her share, sold the residue to the complainant; and that all of them except the said Ann McLaughlin, have conveyed the same to said complainant; that the said Ann McLaughlin is dead, leaving the defendants herein her heirs at law, who

are all non-residents; bill prays that a decree may pass ordering and directing said defendants to convey said land in fee simple to said complainants - S. Archer/Dissolution of partnership of Jacob H. Munnikhuysen and Samuel Gover; the former has removed to house opp Tavern of Stephen Jones, formerly occ as a printing office of Wm. Coale, where he will continue dry goods and grocery business/Fair held by ladies of Chestertown/James Walker, Elkton, answers statments made in earlier issue of The Citizen which assailed him re Mr. Doran, "my father's friend."/Elder James McVey to hold a 2 day meeting at Union Chapel/Mr. Blondel of Balt, to open a Dancing School at the house of Maj. William Richardson/Sale of cow, horse cart, and a lot of land whereon Wm Taylor res, to satisfy two judgments rendered by Samuel Reed, one at the suit of Evan Lloyd, use of Joseph Aston and one at the suit of Nicholas Cooper - Wm. Harrod, Constable

191. ICP Jun 24 1830/Cavalry notice - The 1st Troop of Harford Light Dragoons are to assemble at Patterson's Old Fields - Ethan Michael, Qr. Master Sergt/Sheriff's sale of right of John Boyd to house in Havre-de-Grace, and furniture, horse, cow, at suit of Edward Courtney exec of Jonas Courtney /Trustee's sale of prop called Leigh of Leighton of which Joseph Slee of Balt, died seized, five miles from Bush - John Slee, Trustee/Sale at the Black House Tavern of lands whereon James Meads, decd res at the time of his death, being the lands occ by said James Meads, except 100 a. heretofore sold to Elisha Meads, the part now to be sold, about 120 a. - Otho Scott, trustee /Land for sale whereon Thomas Miles decd res at time of his death, about 100a., now in possession of Joshua Guyton; adj lands of Thomas Hope and Thomas Hutchins - Otho Scott, trustee/For sale in Belle Air, nr Broad Creek called Pearson's Pen, about 250 a./Sheriff's sale of pers prop of Jesse Jarrett at suit of Charles Robinson/Sheriff's sale of est of James Hughes, tract called Friendship, 95 a., use of Richard Mitchell

192. ICP Jul 8 1830/James Porter, one of the mail robbers, was executed at Phila; he was a native of Ireland, age 24/Sale of farm, Sidney Park, in Swan Creek adj est of William Herman Stump, John S. Webster and Mrs. Griffith, 237 a.; also Hall's Purchase and Young Man's Addition, about 230 a., adj Capt Murphy's farm, on Spesutia Narrows and Shandy Hall - Henry Hall, trustee; also a farm, pt of Hall's Purchase and 5 lots in Havre de Grace - Henry Hall, Walter T. Hall, trustees/Lots for sale in Port Deposit at house of James Knight, Innkeeper - John Creswell/$100 reward by W. W. Forwood for scoundrel who broke into his factory, threw down his fences and injured his cattle /Creditors are requested to exhibit claims agns est of George Presbury of William

193. ICP Jul 15 1830/Portion of this issue is missing/Chestertown Telegraph for sale; published 5 yrs

194. ICP Jul 22 1830/Idependent Citizen is published by John M'Kenney Jr and Augustus A. Bond/Otho Scott has resigned his seat in the Executive Council, replaced by John Forwood of Harf Co/Married Thurs evening last by Rev William Kesley, Thomas Knight to Miss Strena(?) Spence, all of this co/Died, Mrs. Margaret Belton, consort of Wiliam Belton, Mon 12 inst, in 72d yr, leaving two daughters; she came to res with her daughters in this village about 15 months past; she was considred by an eminent clergyman of Balt of the most worthy/Died Wed 14 inst at his res in this co, Jacob Balderston, aged 72,

member of Soc. of Friends/Camp Meeting on lands of Henry Webster - William Kesley, Preacher, Harf Co/Farm for sale on which he lives adj Hickory Tavern - Samuel James/Letters remaining at P.O. Darlington: Ann Amos; Elizabeth Cox; Joseph Husband; Lewis T. Pyle; Mary Ann Watkins; Mrs. Watkins; John Wordsworth - Edward J. Markland, Post Master/Samuel Sutton declines candidacy /James Moores and Alexander Norris, candidates for Legislature of Md

195. ICP Jul 22 1830/Letters remaining at P. O. Bel-Air: Miss Laura Archer; Miss J. A. Allen; Mrs. Susan Jane Ashley; George Amos; Agnes Beattie; William Briley; Eliue Brown; Z. O. Bond; Thomas W. Bond; Widow Blake; Thomas Bay; John Bleake; William Coale; Philip Coale; Henry Christie; Henry Connolly; Miss Priscilla Christie; Mrs. Elizabeth Davis; Thomas Dorsey; Dr. Hiram D. Davis; Abel Durham; Dr. Archibald Dorsey; Capt John Elliott; William Edie; Caroline Fisher; Edward M. Guyton; Joshua Guyton; William Glen; James Guyton; Jesse Gilbert; Charles Gorsuch; Thomas Hays; Hanna Harli; Alexander Harper; Miles Hilton; Thomas Hope; Robert J. Henderson; Cheyney Hoskins; Sidney Hall; Thomas Hope; Henry H. Johns; Stephen Jones; Miss Mary Ann Jenkins; Josiah Johnson; Abraham Jarrett; Mrs. Theopilis Jones; John Jewett Jr; John Judd; John Jordan; James Jones; William C. Kirkwood; Sheriff of Harford; Mary Kerr; William Kenney; Daniel Long; Miss Mary M. Lansdale; Martha Lancaster; I. Maulsby; Amos Mccomas; Job Miton; James Magness; John Marshand(?); Lucretia G. Moore; Cloe McAtee (colored woman); Dr. James Montgomery; Ephraim McCleary; James Meade; Mrs. Sarah McCracken; Andrew Miller; John Morrison; William Michael; Samuel Moody; German McClure; James Nelson; Isaac Norris; John C. Norris; Vincent Norris; T. H. Niak; Isaac Pyle Junr; Miss Caroline E. Perryman; Samuel Parkinson; Isaac Preston; Francis Potee; Mr. ___ Prichett; Doctr. A. Preston; John W. Rutledge; Thomas T. Richardson; Ann Reese; John Rodgers; Vincent Richardson; Isaac Robinson; Joshua Rutledge; Messrs Jno and Thomas Smithson; Esther S,. Smithson; Abraham Stanley; Col. John Street; Mrs. Elizabeth Smithson; Mrs. Mary Smithson; William Smithson; Richard C. Stockson; Otho Scott; Charles S. Sewell; John Sharp; Sarah Sykes; John Scarf; Mrs. Hannah A. Scott; John Tredway; Henry Tuchstone; Joseph Turner; Miss Rosa Vincent; Henry Woolsey; Mrs. Martha Webster; Jonathan Warner; Benjamin N. Wells; John Wann; Thomas Ward; Miss Elizabeth Wheeler; Lloyd Williams; Joshua Whitaker - John Robinson, P.M/John H. Price Atty at Law at his office in Bel-Air on Mon and Tues; remainder of week at William Wilson's nr Darlington

196. ICP Jul 29 1830/Thomas Hope declines candidacy/Stephen Watters and Capt Henry P. Ruff, candidates for Legislature of Md/Died Sat 17 inst, James Maxwell Day, only son of late James M. Day of Gunpowder Neck, after a lingering illness of much suffering/Runaway negro man, Henry Bell; says he is prop of Richard Pyle of Montgomery Co; he is about 24-25, 5 ft 9-10 inch

197. ICP Aug 4 1830/The ladies' Fair yielded $600; walls were covered with drapery, evergreen and flowers; tables covered with every article which taste or fancy could devise/Married Thurs evening last by Rev Richardson, Benjamin Magness to Miss Sarah Eliza Magness, all of this co/Dr. James Montgomery candidate for Gen Assembly/Land for sale, about 300 a., on Deer Creek - Samuel Forwood of Jno

198. ICP Aug 19 1830/Population of our town according to latest census is 334/Court case - breach of promise of marriage - Miss Ann Wade agnst Charles R. Cockey in 1827 in Balt Co Court and removed to this co; $3,300 damages awarded for plaintiff; Levin Gale, Albert Constable and William H. Collins for

plaintiff and John Scott, I. D. Maulsby and Otho Scott for defendant /Married 12 inst by Rev Finney, John Scott of Mt Pleasant, Ohio, to Miss Rebecca Beatty of this co/Married in Phila 23 Jun by Rev Boyd, James Davis, formerly of this co, to Louisa dau of Lewis Desague/Died Tues eve last at res of his father in this co, Charles Penrose Hall, youngest child of Walter T. Hall; 9 summers only witnessed the growth of this flower/Committed to jail, runaway negro man, Charles; he says he belongs to Sheppard C. Leakin of Balt; he is about 5 ft 5 inch, 19-20, light complexion/Cash for good seasoned flour barrels at Patterson's Mills, Gunpowder Falls - Z. Rhodes/Stray buffaloe cow came to plantation of Ebenr. N. Allen, in Broad Neck/Sale at his res on Water's Run nr Coop's Town: horses, cattle, hogs, ox cart, farming utensils, furniture, carpenters tools and other items and tract of 110 a. - Joel Brown

199. ICP Aug 26 1830/Newspaper, The Harford Republican and People's Advocate has been established, supporting Pres Jackson/Married Tues 17 inst by Rev Stansbury Galion, William Smith to Miss Julia Ann Brown, all of this co/Died, Catharine Brown, aged 26, dau, sister and friend/Died Sat 14 inst at res of John Hopkins in this co, Philip G. Gover, late of Balt, in 37th yr/Died at Blenheim, his late res in this co, yesterday morning, 25 inst, Paca Smith /Albert Constable requests claims agnst est of late Dr. John Archer be exhibited

200. ICP Sep 2 1830/Died Mon evening Aug 23 after a long illness, William Loflin, 56, leaving wife and large family of children/Died same day in her father's house, Mary, dau of Above decd, in 20th yr, of bilious fever /Equity case - Joel Carter vs John Wood, Pa; bill states that complainant and John Wood as tenant in common were seized of tract in Harf Co called Bond's Last Shift, about 500 a., and mutually agreed on a division of prop. One full column in this issue decribes bonds and payments to be paid. Carter acuses Wood of fraud in obtaining a judgement in Harf Court agnst him

201. ICP Sep 9 1830/Married Tues evening 31 ult by Rev Parke, John Young to Miss Mary Pyle, both of this co/Married Tues evening last by Rev Stevenson, William Lawrence to Miss Jemima Tutchstone, all of this co/Died Tues morning 24 ult in 49th yr of her age, Susan West, consort of Stacy West, after a painful illness/Camp meeting on land of Morris Malsby, 1 miles form Davis' saw mill and about 1 miles form David Newlin's mill/Meeting of candidates at Tavern of Benjamin B. Amos (late Carman's)/Dr. Thomas C. Hopkins, can be found at res of Amos Gilbert except when absent on professional duties

202. ICP Sep 16 1830/Married Tues evening last by Rev Finney, James Jeffery, of Pittsburg, Pa, to Miss Jane A., eld dau of John Anderson, of this co /Married Tues morning last in this town by same, Benjamin Silver Jr to Mrs. Hannah Morgan, all of this co/Thomas Archer, Atty at Law, has office in Bel-Air (formerly occ by Judge Archer)/Commission to divide and survey a road between road leading from the Hickory to the Trap and the road from the first mentioned place to Conowingo Bridge on a direction from Parker's Mill to Watters Meeting House on Thomas Run - Henry G. Watters, Mathew Cain, William Pyle/Constable's sale at suit of Patrick McDonnel, use of Joel Brown, right of Harry Gilbert to tract in Harf Co nr Upper Cross Roads on which William Logue now res - John Scarff, Constable/Samuel Stone, Balt Co, offers reward for negroes: Dan, about 29, about 5 ft 9 inch; Josh, mulatto, about 28, about 5 ft 6 inch; Peter, mulatto, about 20, about 5 ft 8 inch; Mariam, black woman, about 21, about 5 ft 9 inch

203. ICP Sep 30 1830/Henry Dorsey of Edward, Bel-Air, offers reward for negroes: Dinah, about 52, black; Caroline dau of Dinah, about 34; 3 sons of Caroline, Bob, 12; Philip, 10, and Joe, 8; Charles, about 21; Harriet, sister of Charles, about 23/Henry P. Ruff prevented by indisposition and not yet recovered, declines candidacy/Elders, C. Furguson and J. Henshaw, will hold a meeting in the Union Chapel on third Sabbath Oct next/For sale - House now occ by Mrs. Billingslea; store house lately occ by Messrs Gover and Munnickhuysen, farm occ by Jason Thompson - Jason Moore/Sheriff's sale of right of Charles Gilbert of Michael to tracts, Clark's Tobacco, Union, Obadiah's Venture, The Improved Adventure, Gilbert's Pipe, Jack's Purchase, Doubloon - 400 a., being lands devised to him by his grandfather, Charles Gilbert, at suit of James Stephenson/Sheriff's sale of right of Luther A. Norris to tract in Bush River Neck, 281 3/4 a., being lands devised to the wife of Luther A. Norris by Clark Hollis, decd, at suit of John Johnson and Edward Grifith/For rent - house in this village, lately occ by Mrs. Wagner opp post office - Thomas A. Hays/Sale of real est of Martha Dorset: Lot No. 3 adj lands of Abner Gilbert, within 3 miles of Hall's Cross Road

204. ICP Oct 7 1830/Died Fri last, Mrs. Mary Matthews, consort of John C. Matthews, of this co/A sermon will be preached by Rev Tippet on the death of Mr. Loflin and his two daughters, at the house of Mrs. Loflin nr the res of Thomas Jeffery, Fri 29th at 10 o'clock/Examinations at Abingdon Academy - John C. Norris, Sec'ry/Margaret Smith adm of Paca Smith, to sell at Blenheim, pers est of decd, including 1 two-horse carriage, gig, sulky carts, large wagon, farming utensils, extensive library; and balance of prop at farm on the Cranberry

205. ICP Oct 14 1830/Married Tues evening 5 inst by Rev John R. Keech, William Ashdown, to Miss Sarah Lemon/Died 6 inst, Samuel Hopkins, member of Soc. of Friends, in 55th yr/Died at her res in Balt Co Sat 2d in 31st yr, after a short but severe indisposition, Mrs. Eliza B. Grupy, consort of Jacob Grupy, leaving husband and 5 small children/Letter to Dr. R. N. Allen regarding his recent expressions of support to the adminsitration of Pres. Jackson/A colt has strayed from Ch'r Wilson, nr Darlington

206. ICP Oct 21 1830/Married Tues evening 12 inst by Rev Huing, Samuel Webb to Miss Mary Street, both of Harf Co/Died in City of Washington, Sun, 10 inst, after a short illness, Mrs. Sarah Coale, consort of William Coale, former editor of Bond of Union, in 49th yr, leaving husband and 8 children /Died Wed night 13 inst at the res of Ephraim Swartz in the village of Abingdon in this co, Miss Elizabeth Jones/Died at Annapolis Fri last, Colonel William Done, Delegate elect to Legislature of Md from Som So/William Billingslea res 21 miles from Balt on Phila Turnpike Road, offers reward for negro girl, Mary, 16-17, 5 ft 5-6 inch; had on an iron collar which she can hide with her handkerchief; took with her several changes of dress

207. ICP Nov 4 1830/Margaret Herbert adm of John Herbert/Marrried Thurs last by Rev Finney, James Riley to Miss Matilda Wareham, all of this co/John Chauncey adm of Cornelius Coale to sell balance of est of decd/William McJilton insolvent debtor disch from imprisonment/Letters remaining at P.O. Darlington: Major John Amos, Doct. Robert Archer, John Brennan (cooper), L. E. Cassidy, Capt ___ Johnson - E. J. Markland, P.M.

208. ICP Nov 11 1830/Died in this co Sat 30 ult in 69th yr, Mrs. Mary Norris, relict of Aquila Norris, wife and mother/Mount Ararat Lodge No. 44 of Free Masons, will sit at their new hall in Bel-Air - I. D. Maulsby, Sec'ry /Sale of prop of R. H. Douglas in pursuance of his will, tract in Harf Co, 209 a., nr res of Morris Malsby. Plat may be seen at Counting House of R. H. Douglas and Co. No. 50 South Gay St. - Silas Marean, James I. Fisher, exec /Sale by trustees of Luther A. Norris, insolvent debtor, of Balt Co, of his title to tract in Harf Co, called Elling, pt Swampy Point, pt of Holly Hill, pt Islington, pt Planter's Neglect, pt Parker's Folly, pt Holling Refuge and pt Hanson's Regnedged Neck - 280 a. - H. W. Bool Jr, auct./Jehu Smith ofers for sale farm where he res, about 160 a., about 5 miles of Conowingo bridge

209. ICP Nov 18 1830/Married Thurs 11 inst by Rev Parke,Lewis Pyle of this co to Ann Johnson of Balt City/Married 12 inst at Friends Meeting House, Deer Creek, Abraham Conard, of Lancater Co, to Ann Coale of this co/Legoe's Point for sale, the farm where he res, at mouth of Bush River - Thomas Bolster/New Fall goods - dry goods and groceries - Ezekiel Morrison has opened a new store in the house nr Herbert's Cross Roads, formerly occ by Mr. McCluskey - will sell at Balt prices/Constable's sale of right of L. Cadwalader Jones to tract Whortleberry Hills, deeded to him by his father, Aquila Jones; also cow, calf, heifer, and 4 sheep, goods and chattels of Sarah Smith - James Harvey, late constable

210. ICP Nov 25 1830/For sale - at Havre de Grace, the Float (for taking fish) heretofore occ by them, with all apparatus belonging thereto - John Donahoo Coin/Former Sheriff's sale of right of William Liggit to tract called Norfolk, 265. a., at suit of Thomas Ayres and Isaac Hitchcock

211. ICP Dec 2 1830/Meeting of Union Temperance Soc. at Blackberry Academy nr Herbert's Cross Roads; elected: Stevenson Archer, pres.; Henry G. Watters, vice pres.; Joseph S. Travelli, sec'y & treasurer/Married Thurs evening last by Rev J. R. Keech, Samuel Ecoff Jr to Miss Susanna Wann, all of this co/Died Mon 22 ult at the res of Sam'l M'Gay, Mrs. Hannah Hanna, relict of Alexander Hanna, in 80th yr/Sheriff's sale of right of James Taylor to tract, Good Speed, 100 a. and a lot at Boothly Hill, 2 a. at suit of William W. Webster /Sheriff's sale of negro women, Patty and Nancy, farming utensils, furniture, goods and chattels of George Griffith, at suit of Isaac Perryman assigneee of John Johnson and Thomas Wilson/A black reticle lost between Col Dorsey's gate and Binam's runs; finder may keep money if left with Stephen Jones, Bel-Air /George William Hall, Constable, Friendship, Harf Co, wishes to hire 6 farm hands for next year

212. ICP Dec 9 1830/Married Wed evening 1 inst by Rev Tippet, Kent Chesney, to Miss Jane Price, all of this co/Trustees of the Poor, will sell prop now occ by Alms House, about 50 a./Jesse Hollingsworth, Benjamin Baxter, William Baxter, Harf Co, insolvent debtors, disch from imprisonment

GENERAL INDEX

ABBOTT Meliscent 1,49; William F. 1, 39, 49
ABINGDON Fair 182
Abraham Choice 18
Abraham's inheritance 127, 166
ABRAHAMS J. W. 71
ADAMS William 111
Addition to Brother's Lot 98
Addition to New Hall 17
Addition to Ward's Intent 173
ALDERSON Abel 154
ADY James 95; Samuel 94, 102, 137; Solomon 102
AIRS Samuel W. 95
AKINS William 16
ALBERT Joseph 111
ALBERTSON Jonathan 10, 13
ALBETT Dew. 111
ALDRIDGE John 41; Margerey 81
ALLEN James 55
ALEXANDER & MORROW 34
ALEXANDER Alexander 6, 59, 65, 79; Andrew 15; James 132, 177; John 103; Josiah 39; Letticia 59; Levi 59; Ma... 95; Mary 59; Mary E. 59; Richard F. 18, 36, 37, 39, 79, 86, 87; Robert 18; Tamison 37
Alexander's Lot 9
ALISON R., M. D. 91
ALLEN Capt John 92; Dr. 142; Dr. R. N. 109, 147, 181, 189, 205; Dr. Richard N. 110; Ebenezer N. 132, 198; Edward E. 134; Hannah 16; Isaac 94; John 111; Miss J. A. 195; R. N. 95, 97, 103, 106; Reuben 133; Rev John 180; Robert 34; William 16, 132, 177; William H. 131
ALLENDER Nicholas 115; George 115
ALLISON Andrew 34
ALLSTON Samuel C. 15
Alms House 212
Amos & Myers Puzzle 143
AMOS Alexander 177; Ann 194; Aquila 111; Benjamin B. 201; Bradford 111; Capt John Archer 187; Elizabeth 133, 179; Frederick T. 111; Frederick Taylor 146; George 111, 195; George R. 176; James 116, 133; James B. 110, 111, 132; John 133; John A. 177; John T. 100; Joshua M. 173; Joshua of Robert 177; Lieut James B. 187; Major

Frederick T. 102; Major John 207; Oliver H. 131; Temperance 106, 133; William of James 131; William S. 94
AMOSS Benj... 95; Benjamin B. 147; F. T. 110; Isaac R. 176; John Archer 183; Sarah E. 176; William 100; William of James 105
ANAUDAIN John 29
Anchor and Hope 13
ANDERSON Eleanor 36; George 13, 68; Jacob 72; Jane A. 202; John 177, 181, 202; Moses 130; Susan 53
ANDREWS Henry 8, 82; James 2, 49, 54
ANGIER Unit 62
Antrim 94
Aquila's Inheritance 98, 107
Arabia Petre 98
Arabia Petrea 101
ARCHER Dr. John 167, 199; Dr. R. H. 116, 136, 183; Dr. Robert 207; Hannah S. 167; John 94, 98, 106, 118, 127, 143, 150, 169; Judge 107, 202; Laura 195; Robert H. 134, 159; S. 150, 190; Stevenson 4, 97, 100, 103, 128, 161, 183, 211; Thomas 202
ARCHIBALD William 21
ARMSTRONG Andrew 7
ARNAT William 58
ASH Jacob 35, 89; John 53, 59, 87; Ruth 15
ASHDOWN Mary 133; W. 189; William 116, 205
ASHLEY Susan Jane 195
ASHTON Edward 95; Richard 177
ASKEW Hannah 92
ASTON Joseph 190
ATHERTON Robert 79; William 105
ATKINSON Charlotte 96; Israel 136
AUSTEN Rachel 92
AUSTIN James 10; James O. 10
AUX Elizabeth 28
AYRES Thomas 100, 104, 126, 127, 133, 143f, 168, 171, 183, 210; Thomas W. 94

Back Creek Mills 73
BACKUM John 53
BACON Capt Daniel 30
BADGER Mescus M. 30
BAGELEY John O. 164; Mrs. 105
BAGGOT Thomas 144
BAGLEY George 111; John O. 111
BAIER John 134
BAILEY Mary 113, 127

-57-

BAKER Abraham 173; Elizabeth 172; Graftin 111; Henry 15; Jacob 75; James 116, 183; Jeremiah 168; Nicholas 108; Samuel 79
BALDERSON Ely 61; Jacob 111
BALDERSTON Jacob 95, 194
Baldfrier Ferry 1
BALDWIN Marshall 98; Silas 98
Baldwin's & Ashton Innocence 143
BALL David 79; George 32
BARCLAY John 133
Barclay's Old Field 110
BARE Samuel 98
BARNES Elizabeth 31; Hosea 99; Hosier 132, 177; Isaac 111; Lydia 104, 127, 171, 180; Patrick 43; William 189
Barnes Delight 98
Barnes Neglect 98
Barnes Neighborhood 98
BARNETT Elizabeth 169, 173; William 28
BARNEY John H. 150; Margaret 150
BARR Samuel 77
BARRATT Rev Andrew 71
BARRELL William H. 57
BARRET John 96
BARRETT Andrew 87
BARROLL William H. 55
BARROT William H. 36
BARSEN Samuel 96
BARTOL George 51, 134, 182
BARTON Mr 86
BATES John 79
BAXTER Benjamin 116, 212; Benjamin H. 169; Jacob 165; Mr. 116; Samuel 95, 106, 165; William 161, 212; William, Senr 175
BAY Daniel 177; Elizabeth 133; James M. 133; Thomas 177, 195
BAYARD Stephen 87; Thomas 79
BAYLES Zepheniah 108
BAYLESS Mary 167; Zephaniah 132, 189
BAYNARD Nathan 91
BEAL William P. 133
BEANS Jonathan 53; Stephen 43, 48
BEARD Dr. James 14, 68; Hugh 10; J. 10; Lambert 40, 57
BEASTEN George 1, 61; Mr. 63; Mr. Z. 66; Zebulon 4
BEASTON George 11, 19, 87; Mr. 7; Zebulon 21, 37
BEATTIE Agnes 195
BEATTY James 167, 187; Rebecca 198
BEATY Samuel 11
BECHME Charles L. 102

BECK Millisent 62; S. 62
BEEDLE John 36, 53, 59
BEGLEY John A. 11
Bel-Air population 198
Belhaven 33, 88
BELL David 133, 134; Elizabeth 181; Henry 196; Joseph 95; Robert 181; Sarah 133
Bell Tavern 164
Belle Farm 99, 170
Belle Grade 101
BELT George Gordon 34
BELTON Margaret 194
BEMIS N. S. 111; Nathan 151; Nathan S. 124, 129, 132, 136, 149, 177, 182
BENDER Nathaniel 37
BENETT Sarah 117
BENNET Sarah 118
BENNETT A. 34; Abraham 60; Ann 79; Henry 2, 28, 52, 85
BENSON Benjamin 8
BERG Christian 94
BERMINGHAM James 116
BERNARD Parker 59
BERRY John 59, 92
Best Endeavour 101
Betsey's Choice 102
Better Luck 126
Betty's Lot 101
BEVARD Samuel 111
BIDDLE Andrew 85; Augustin 79; Elizabeth 42; George 14; H. L. 72; J. F. A. 65; Jacob 42, 89; John 15, 59; John F. A. 48; Lambert 34; Lambert W. 92; Noble 15; Peregrine 14, 30; Spencer 59, 79, 86, 87; Thomas 2, 7, 40, 51; Thomas A. 85; Tobias 84; Tobias R. 11; William 59
Bilberry hall 161
BILES William B. 27
BILLINGSLEA Bennet M. 188; Elizabeth 115; James 104, 156; Mrs. 203; William 206
Billy's Portion 102
Birchfield's Venture 98
BIRCKHEAD Elizabeth 101
BIRKHEAD Thomas H. 101
BISHOP Stephen 170; William 105
BLACK Charles G. 87; John 36; John N. 6, 11, 31, 168; Sarah 42; William 15
Black's Cross Roads 10
BLACKBURN John 111
BLACKSTON John 173; Rebecca 173
BLAKE John 116, 161; Widow 195

-58-

BLANEY John 116, 183
BLEAKE John 183, 195
BLONDEL Mr. 190
BLOOD Oliver 53
Bloom's Bloom 101
Blue Ball tavern 65
BOHEL Samuel 36
BOLSTER Thomas 209
BOLTIN James 79
BOND Augustus A. 142, 194; Buckler 119; Dr. 103; James 135; John 169; M. T. 176; Nancy 171, 181; Nicholas M. 139; Priscilla Ann 166; Thomas 87, 90; Thomas W. 148, 195; William B. 105, 118, 135; Z. O. 94, 103, 195, 166; Zachariah 124; Zacheus O. 177
Bond of Union (newspaper) 206
Bond's Last Shift 200
Bond's Pleasant Hills 161
BOOL H. W. Jr 208
Boothly Hill 141, 211
BORAM Henry 79; Mary 15
BORDLEY Julian C. 55; William 55
BORELAND Mathew 59
BORTON Capt Solomon 30
BOSLEY James 182
Bottom Meadow 38
BOTTS John 117
BOUCHEL Peter 89
BOUCHELL John 35; Peter 35
BOULDEN Alexander 66; Ann 92; Ann P. 28; Benjamin 40; Jesse 17, 78; Levi 46, 53; Margaret 37; Rachel 28; Richard 11, 17; William 37
BOUSHELL Peter 40
BOWEN Benjamn 32; Robert 95
BOWMAN John L. 59
BOWSER Samuel 14
BOYD John 191; David 36; Rev 198; Stephen 132
BOYER Dr. Henry G. 183; William 42
BRADDOCK George 7
BRADENBAUGH Jacob 132
BRADFIELD Enos 96
BRADFORD A. 186; A. W. 149, 182; Augustus W. 108, 137; Dr. C. H. 189; George 132, 164, 177; George W. 183; Robert 132; Samuel 94, 95, 97, 98, 101, 107, 114, 128, 132, 137, 158, 159, 161, 170, 171, 177, 185, 189
BRADLEY Thomas 58
BRANNAN John 182
BRANNON John 111
BRECKENRIDGE Rev. 187

BRANNAN John 207
BRENT James W. 134
BREVITT Benedict S. 62
Briary Island 169
BRICE Joseph 62
Brick Hill 43
Brick Meeting House 4, 7
BRICKLEY Andrew 21; James H. 11, 37; Jehoackim 25; Jehoiakim 37
Bridge construction 112
BRILEY William 195
BRINTON Edward 103
BRISCO Henrietta 53
BRISCOE Elizabeth 88; Frederick G. 1; John 11; Margaret 62; Samuel 88; Samuel R. 36, 59, 88
BRISLEY Mary 79
BRISTOW Melescent 35
BROMWELL Jacob 16
BROOKS Benjamin 173; Elizabeth 103; George G. 134; William 96, 177
Brother's Discovery 98
Brother's Lot 98
Brotherly Care 167, 187
BROUGHTON James 87
BROWN Capt 134, 149; Catharine 199; Davis S. 1331 Ebenezer 116; Edmond 53; Edmund 79; Eliue 195; Elizabeth 133, 169; Elizabeth M. 124; Freeborn 161; Isaac 90; Isaiah 28; Jacob 110; James H. 134; Jeremiah 14, 69, 104; Jesse 46; Joel 198, 202; John 6, 17, 53, 103; John C. 97; John Porter 34; Joseph 190; Josiah 124; Julia Ann 199; Levin 54; Margaret 6; Mary B. 127, 161; Mrs. 133; Rebecca 36; Samuel 132, 177; Simon 111; Slater 14, 69; Stephen 111; William 2, 14
Brown's Discovery 98, 101
BROWNE James 62
BROWNLEY Joseph 125, 165
BRYAN Albert G. 36; Dr. Guy 44; George 28; James Y. 53; John 46, 53; Joseph 36, 73, 79, 87
BRYANT John 59
BRYARLY Wakeman 108
BRYNAM Thomas 95
BRYNE John 53
BUDD John 110
BULKLEY John 97
BULL Elisha 116; John E. 183; Sarah 173, 183; Walter 88, 130, 173
Bull's Head Tavern 159
BUNTING J. P., Post master 96, 103

BURCHALL Robert 8
BURCHELL Robert 91
BURGAIN Joshua 92
BURGOYNE James 32
BURK Mary Ann 92
BURKINS John of Isaac 111
BURLAGE John 56
BURNS Thomas 11, 87
BURR Mr. 3
BURTON Miers 91
BURTS Margaret 6; Thomas 6, 48
BUSSEY Bennet 94; Dr. 136; Dr. Bennett F. 189; Edward F. 95, 124, 177; Eliza. 183; Elizabeth 101
BUTLER Clement 132; Elijah 89; George H. 36; John 95, 106, 111; Lewis 102, 116, 125; Thomas 94, 125

CAIN Elizabeth 106, 169; John 106; Mathew 202; Mrs. Matthew 124
CAIRNS William 132, 171
CALDEN James 95; Sophia 95
CALDER Lloyd 106
CALDWELL John 111; Thomas 116; Thomas jr 132
CALLENDER William 1
CALVERT William H. 32, 88
CALWEL Eliza 183
CALWELL Thomas 106; Thomas J. 136
CAMERON James 5, 85, 87; John C. 19, 84; Matthew 85; Robert 5, 11
CAMP William 91
CAMPBELL Bing 25; David J. 72, 81; James 168; John 92; Mary 21
CANN Mary 83
CANTWELL Matthew 57
Cantwell's Bridge 13
CAR Jesse 106
CAREINS Robert 97; William 97, 154, 173
CARLILE John W. 96, 147
CARLISLE John W. 157
Carman's Tavern 201
CAROTHERS Francis 79
Carpenter's Point 32, 61
CARR Dabney S. 108; William 95; William, Jr 124
CARROL Aquila 178
CARROLL James 104
CARSINS John 108, 181
CARSON Ann 92
CARTER James 35;Joel 150, 200; Robert 25
CARUTHERS Walter 59

CARY Richard 95
CASHO Jacob 35
CASSIDY L. E. 207
CATON Richard 65
CAULK Oliver 57
CAVENDER Abraham 111
CAZIER Charity 36; John F. 8
Cecil Furnace lands 6
Cecil Mills 182
CHAFTIN Joseph B. 179
CHAMBERLAIN Henry 87; Mr. 53
CHAMBERLAINE Henry 13, 168
CHAMBERLIN James 7, 63; Lewis 60
CHAMBERS Benjamin B. W. 71; E. F. 33; Nicholas 53, 71; Rebecca 53; Rev 7, 57
Chambers Venture 32
CHAMPAN John 41
CHANCE Mary Ann 28, 80
CHANY Richard 30
CHAPEL Robert 124
Charles Bounty 100
Charles Neighbor 100
CHAUNCEY John 121, 126, 134, 167, 183, 207
Cheek's Old Field 31
CHERLS Joseph 111
CHESNEY Kent 212
CHESNUT Jared 9
Chestertown Fair 190
CHEW Ann W. 62; Edward 111; William M. 114
CHEYNER Edith 124
CHEYNEY Edith 133
CHICK Jesse 15; Josiah 59
CHRISTFIELD Gilbert 7
CHRISTIE Henry 165, 195; Priscilla 195
CHRISTOPHER John 106
CHURCHMAN George 7
Churchtown 66
Clackstone's Forrest 154
CLARK Capt William 106; Jane 28; Martha Ann 181; Ralph 132; Sarah 53; Thomas 95; William 124
Clark's Dunmurry 94
Clark's Tobacco 203
CLARKSON Levy 92; Mrs. Leonard 116
Claxton's Forest 140
CLAYLAND Mary E. H. 79
CLAYTON Eliza 79; Mary E. H. 15; Thomas D. 41
CLEAVELAND Dr. 71
CLENDENIN John 133; Sarah E. 116
CLENDINEN Sarah E. 183; John 169
CLIFTON William H. 59

CLINE Jacob 169
CLOTHIER William Kirk 11
CLOUD Charles F. 84; Dr. Caleb W. 28; Enoch 7, 35, 87; Josseph 81
CLOWARD Mary Ann 34
CLOWES Rev Dr. 75; Rev T. 83
CLYME Jacob 15; John 15; Philip 15
COAL Mary C. 96; William 10
COALE & PENINGTON 74
COALE Amelia S. 53; Ann 53, 209; Anne 5; Cornelius 207; Dr. S. H. 116; Maria 53; Philip 195; Richard 177; Sarah 206; Skipwith 5, 52; Wiliam 139, 51, 183, 190, 195, 206; William S. 87
COATS Mathias 51
COBURN William 44
COCHLEN Capt Rendel 16
COCHRAN Col. James 168; James 36, 175; John 16; John T. 35
COCKEY Charles R. 198
COCKRAN Thomas 18; William 18
COE Peter 83
COIN John Donahoo 210
COLDWELL John 28
COLE Cornelius 167; Jacob 80; James 95, 111; Rev 13; William 111
Colegate's Last Shift 102
COLEMAN Charles 50; Isaiah 55, 62
COLINS James 9; Jesse 134; William H. 198
COLMARY William 59
COMEGYS John 39; John W. 5, 58
Common garden 99, 169
CONARD Abraham 209; William 50
Concord 40
CONKEY John H. 79, 84
CONNELLY Elizabeth 106
CONNER Ann 79
CONNOLLY Henry 195
Conowingo Fair 66
CONRAD J. 4, 60; Jacob 42; John 1, 4, 42, 46, 60
Consent 4, 32
CONSTABLE Albert 107, 131, 141, 152, 156, 167, 171, 198, 199
Constable Manor 100
Constant Friendship 164
Contestible Manor No. 2 101
Contrivance 187
Convenience 127
CONWAY Dr. 106; John 5; William D., M. D. 103
COOK Samuel 116
Cook's Rest and Royal Exchange 178

COOLEY Carvil 39; Daniel M. 9; Daniel M. 171, John 9; Lawson 25
COOPER Basil 183; Elizabeth 183; Francis 183; Henry 183; Isaiah 12, 13, 34, 61, 147; John M. 154; Mary 183; Nathaniel 183; Nicholas 95, 133, 135, 147, 190; Philip 183; Samuel 74; W. 34; William 116
COPPIN John 48
CORBLEY Richard 59
CORD Amos 103, 121
CORKS George 62
CORSE James 89; Mary 70; Mary P. 89; Unit 89
COSDEN G. B. 44, 63; Jeremiah 35, 36, 45, 59, 72, 84; Joseph 40
COSGROVE William 30
COTTINGHAM Sarah 91
COUPER James 91
Court House Point 4, 40, 89
COURTNEY Edward 104, 191; Hanson 177; Jonas 104, 191; Thomas 98, 177; Thomas Jr 101; Thomas sen. 101
COVINGTON Samuel 8, 62
COWAN Robert 179; William 3, 5, 58, 87
COX Dinah 16 Elizabeth 194; Israel 99, 139; Joseph 62; Joseph H. 99, 111, 139; Larkin 94; Mary 99; Nicholas 99; Nicholas H. 111; Phebe 96
COXE Major John J. 67
CRADDOCK Benedict 5, 87
CRAGE Nancy 15
CRAIG Alex 28; Alexander 37; Gertrude 5; James 87; Joshua 37; Mary 35, 71; William 40; William Jr 35, 71
CRAM Samuel 53
Cranberry Hill 105
Cranberry Mill 130
CRAWFORD John W. 97; Rebecca 59; William 36; William, sen 28
CRESWELL John 16, 23, 34, 71, 89, 192
CREW Jonas 62; Jonathan 62
CRISTY Robert 23
CROMPTON Helen 53
CROMWELL John Hammond 1
CROOSHANKS Reese 17
CROPPIN John 1
Crops, condition of 143
CROSGROVE John 74
CROSS David 81
CROSSMAN Bishop S. 62
CROUCE Mr. 25
CROUCH Daniel 40; Hannah 1; Robert 1

-61-

CROW John 35; William 35; William, sen 26
CRUTHERS John A. 59
CULEY Carvel 96
CULLEY Archibald 116, 124
CULLOM Daniel 95
CUMMINGS James, sen 28
CUNNINGHAM Andrew 111; Daniel 177; Daniel M 109, 173; George 105; James 111; Mary 79; Mortimore 168; Rachel 163; Thomas 111; W. H. 102
CURRAN Brice 57
CURRY James 100; John 185; Mr. 95; Robert 92

D..BO Levy 106
DAGG Margaret 116
DAILY Martha 143; Thomas 143
DALLAM Dr. William 96; Dr. William M. 108; Francis J. 101, 157; Josias W. 101; Susan 103; Susan R. 183; William M. 94, 101
DAMSEL William 92
DANN Underwood 25
DARE Rev 56
DARRAUGH Martha 173
DAUGHERTY John 169; John D. 116
DAVID Davidson 63
DAVIDGE Dr. John Beale 150
DAVIDSON George 52, 54, 59, 63; John H. 4; Letitia 6; William 6
DAVIS Abel C. 75; Abraham 79; Charles A. 134; Dr. Elijah 132; Dr. Hiram D. 195; Edward 35; Elisha 179; Eliza 18; Elizabeth 195; G. 95; George 37, 103; George C. 111; James 53, 198; John 105; Joseph 107, 108, 177; Joseph jr 132; R. H. 177; Rachel 118; Rev Reuben H. 169; Samuel 6; Sarah 18; William 40
Davis' saw mill 201
DAWNING James R. 79
DAWSON Mr.57; Samuel 43; Thomas S. 59
DAY Goldsmith 132; J. 98; James M. 196; James Maxwell 196; John Y. 155, 169; Joshua 114; William 111
DEAL Lydia 15
DEAN John 53
DEAVER Margaret 190; Richard of James 97
DELACOUR & GAULT 57
DELECOURSE & GAULT 40
DELECOURSE James 40
DELMAS Francis 115, 132, 177; Theodore 99, 168
Delph Farm 101
DEMOSS Thomas 111; William 159
DENBOW Ann 133; Elizabeth 169; Levi 124; Martin 183
DENISON William 79
DENNING Leige 36
DENNY J. E. 78; John E. 78
DESAGUE Lewis 198; Louisa 198
DEVER George of Richard 111; Harman of Richard 111; Hugh 152; James of Richard 111; Thomas 111
DEVOE John 95; Joseph 176
DICKERMAN Henry 30; William 16
DINCLE Peter 127
DINSMORE & KYLE 19
DIOTT James 62
DISBOROUGH Mr. 17
DISNEY Mr. 182
Ditch Meadows 127
DIVERS Ananias 177
DODSON Capt William 103
Dogwood Run 88
DOMINIQUE Thomas 79
DONAHER John 183
DONAHOO Aquila 103; John 210
DONALDSON W. B. 34; William 28
DONE Colonel William 206
DONN J. M. 106; John 102, 104, 132, 165, 177, 180; John M. 103; T. C. 106
DORAN Ann 175; Bennet 132; Mr. 190
DORNEY Thomas 120, 123, 183
DORSET Martha 203
DORSEY Col 211; Dr. A. 124, 133; Dr. Archibald 106, 116, 177, 183, 195; Henry 95, 112, 133; Henry of Edward 166; Henry of Henry 203; Joshua H. 11, 15; Mathew 101; Stephen H. 29; Thomas 195; Thomas J. 134; William F. 36
Doubloon 203
DOUGHERTY Dennis 9; Hugh 32, 79
DOUGHTY Hugh 90; William 90
DOUGLAS R. H. 208
DOVE William G. 177
DOWNER Jason Brown 125
DOWNING Araminta 92; James R. 92; Samuel 6
DRAPER A. C. 92; D. 92
Drew's Enlargment 127, 152
DUCKET Robert L. 28
DUFFIELD George 10, 58; Henry 10
DUKE Rev 52, 66; William 53
DUN John 96
DUNBAR and FOSTER 8

-62-

DUNBAR Andrew 4, 60, 86, 91; Justus 17, 18. 91
DUNCAN ___ 187; Benjamin W. 114, 118; James 173, 177; John 114, 118, 132
Dunkard's harbor 127
DUNN Andrew 25; John 51; John M. 102; Rev Thomas 74; Richison 92
DUNNAHAY James W. 134
DURHAM Abel 195
DUVALL Jennette 169
DYSART Catharine 36; Miss C. 92

EADES Margaretta 62
EAGAN James 87
EARLE Richard 3
EAST James 25; James H. 16
EATON David 111
ECOFF Samuel 95; Samuel Jr 211
EDGAR Agnes 131
EDIE William 195
EDMONDSON Caleb 7; John 19. 89
EDMUNDSON Caleb 87
EDWARD Mr. 116
EDWARDS Alfred P. 96; Teresa 169; William 84
EGBERT Abraham 4
EGE Oliver 134
EGNER Jacob 17; Margaret 92
EGNOR Catherine 53; Jacob 36
Eigh Trap 118
ELDERKIN John 133
ELETT William 62
ELI William 111
ELIAS Elizabeth 59; Jonas 28, 92
ELIASON Elijah 5; Elizabeth 36; John H. 31; Mary 29
ELICOTT Evan T. 182
ELIOTT William M. 183
ELIT William 111
Elkton Forge Com. 10
ELLICOT Evan T. 129
Elling 208
ELLIOTT Capt John 195; Robert 43
ELLISS George W.144; Rowland 2, 17, 43; Samuel 134
ELY Isaac J. 169; Jacob 187; Margaret 126; Moses 36; Mr. 135; William 187
EMMONS Edward 71, 87; Ira 6, 14, 25, 30
Endeavour Cotton Factory 13, 68
ENGLAND Elizabteh 129; John 106, 124; Joseph 14, 69
ENLOWS James 100, 116; John 100; Thomas M. 100

Enterprize Furnace 151
EPINETT Rev L. 28
ETHERINGTON John W. 19
EVANS Amos A. 14, 35; David 28; Edmund 133; Eliza 34; Hugh W. 98; John 35, 36; John of John 11; John R. 85; Kitty 92; L. H. 52, 67, 168; Levi H. 2, 16, 35 52; 61; Major John R. 21; Margaret 79; Mary W. 78, 85; Evans Robert of James 87
EVAT John jr 132
EVATT John sen 99, 111, 167, 187
EVERET Joseph 108
EVERIOTT Lawrence 62
EVERITT Temperance 62; William 183
EWING George 111; James 36, 54; James P. 35; John 87; Rev 175, 177
Ewing's Contrivance 161

Fair 197
Fairbanks Capt 59
Falling Branch, The 171
Fanny's Inheritance 101, 147
FARIS Jacob 54
FARMER Richard 111; William 111
FARRA Susannah 15
FARRY Dennis O. 79
FASQUET William H. 169
FEINCOUR Thomas 106
FELLEN John 111
FENN Abijah 65
FERGUSON John 148
FEROT Ann B. 71
FERRY Dennis O. 53
FERY Dennis 92
FICKEY John 134
FIFE Robert 101
FINEGAN Patricious 81; Patricus 32
FINLAY Rev 137
FINNEY Rev 196, 202, 207; Rev W. 164; Rev William 157, 167; William 183
FISH Rebecca 169; Robert 169
FISHER Andrew 58; Caroline 195; Elizabeth 133; James I. 208
Fisher's Mill 4
FITZE William 105
FLEAHARTY Thomas 177
FLEEHARTY Joshua 111; William 111
FLINTHAM John M. 26, 87
FLOURS D. 133
FOALY Morice 183
FOARD Andrew 9; Charles T. 11; Edward L. 34; Gen. Hezekiah 39, 41; H. Jr 92; Hezekiah 9, 87; Hezikiah Jr 87; John

B. 105; Josiah L. 28, 87; Samuel B. 92; Thomas 177
FOOTE Lewis H. 77, 78
FORD Edward 18; Elizabeth 36; George 38; Isaac 189; Jacob 133; James, P.M. 29; John 173; John B. 161; Rev Charles T. 169; Sally 96; Samuel 25; T. 61
FOREMAN Samuel 124; William 33, 62
FOREWOOD Rheubin 183; William 183
FORREST Josiah 134
FORSTER Francis 65
FORSYTHE George 111; Joseph 111; William 111
FORWARD Jacob 133; John 169
FORWOD Dr. Parker 146; Hannah 138; Harriet 146; Jacob of John 128; John 104, 132, 134, 138, 169. 177. 179, 185, 194; John C. 132, 177; Lydia 124; Mary 95; Samuel 135, 176; Samuel of John 197; W. W. 192; William 169; William W. 105
FOSTER Jackson C. 59; John 95; Moses 133; Thomas 7
FOWLER Ann 96
FOX Samuel 33; Thomas 15, 28
FOXLOW Joseph 46
FOY Henry 133
Fragment, the 100
FREEMAN Dr. A. M. 30; Dr. Clarkson 107; Isaac 51; S. 60; S. H. 69. 79; Samuel 73; Samuel H. 9. 59
FRENCH Ryer M. 30
French's Lot 126
FREY John 35
Frey's Forge 72
FRICK William 108
Friends Discovery 102
Friendship 101. 118, 143, 191, 211
FRISBY Richard 108; Stephen 165
FRY Joseph 148
FRYE Joseph 105
FULFORD Wiliam 145
FULLARD Henry 111, 178
FULLER Joshua C. 177
FULLERTON Rev M. L. 161; Sophia 169. 182
FULTON Alexander 3; Jane 37; John 90; Matilda 150; Thomas 4; William 28, 37, 59, 150
FUNK Gilbert 169
FURGUSON C. 203; John 111
FURNESS Gardner 82

GABBY Jane 161; Joseph 161
GALBREATH John 111, 132, 134
GALE Levin 63, 198; Mr. 84; Rasin 44; Sarah 59; Thomas 87
GALION Stansbury 199
GALLAWAY James 32
GALLOWAY James 99
GALLION Henrietta 121; James 93
GANGEL C. F.79
GARDENER William 79
GARETT William 14
GARNOR William 53
GARRET Learnerd 96; Thomas 9
GARRETT Abraham 169; Jacob R. 92; Mr. 169; William 68
GARRISON James 126; Susannah 126
GASKINS James 154
GAVER Robert 95
GEFERISON 82
GEORGE Joseph 79; William 48, 81
GERE John A. 134
GERRITSON Richard 64
GERRY & KERR 59
GERRY James 11, 19, 23, 44; William 59
GIBBS Hannah 34; Isaac 53
GIBSON Abraham 133, 169; John L. 121
GILBERT Abner 102, 143, 182, 203; Amos 201; Amos, Sen 113; Ann 140; B. 106; Charles 177; Charles of Michael 203; E. W. 83; Elizabeth 157; Harry 202; Henry R. 140; Jervis 156; Jesse 195; Shadrick R. 95, 140; Thomas 15
Gilbert's Pipe 140, 203
GILDEN Reuben 105
GILDER Chs.116
GILES Ann M. 59; Cordelia 134; Hester Ann 116; John R. 59; Thomas 63, 92; William F. 147
GILL George M. 28, 104, 187
GILLASPIE Thomas 111; William 111
GILLASPY Maj. George 88
GILLESPIE Francis 3, 5; James 14, 82; Samuel 45; Thomas H. 132
GILLETT Dr. J. 131
GILLINGHAM Elizabeth 176; Moses 10, 53
GILLISPIE George 87
GILMORE Capt David 14; Capt Samuel 13; David 13; Samuel 19, 89; Sarah 14
GILPIN Henry H. 84; Joseph 15, 50; W. H. 92; William 34
Gilpin's Mill 84
GLADDEN Jacob 103, 111; Jacob Jr 189, 183; James 127; William 95, 105, 106, 124; William, Jr 162

GLADDIN William 111
GLASSGOW Dr. James 142; Elizabeth 142
GLEN William 195
GLENN Elias 75; J. 43; Jefferson 46, 50, 52; John 34; Robert 169; William 116, 132, 177
GLOVER Captain 131
GOFORTH Rev John 118
Good Neighborhood 107
Good Speed 211
GOODEN John 92
GOODING John 83
GORDON Agness 100; Andrew 129; Archibald 8, 56, 59; Francis 31; Gilbert 103; John 36; Lydia 15
GORREL Crawford 183
GORRELL James 37; Lawson 111; Mary 37; Neiper 25; Thomas 95
GORSUCH Charles 195
GOTTIER Francis 7
GOUGH Harry D. 93, 107, 132, 177
GOVER & MUNNICKHUYSEN 203
GOVER Elizabeth 171; Ephraim G. 171; James 111, 177; James P. 132; Jarrett 171; Margaretta 171; Mr. 186; Philip G. 199; Philip R. 171; Robert 111, 113, 171, 175; Robert of Philip 109, 113; Samuel 145, 190
Gover's Mill 185
GRAFTON Aquila 127; Aquilla 125; Basil 177; John 127; Mary Ann 125; William 133
GRAHAM B. 87;Samuel 19; Thompson 16
Gravely Hills 178
GRAVES John G. 62; William H. 92
Great Britain 101, 127
GREEN Cassandra 169; Clara 176; Clement 130, 147, 179; Ellen 131; John 106; John M. 183; John W. 188; Richard 79; Thomas 106; William 106, 133
Green Hill 23
GREENWOOD Jona 79; Jonathan 15, 29
GREEVES Edward 59
GREME A. I. 133; A. J. 95; Mary 106
GRIFFEN Sabus 79
GRIFFIN Thomas 101, 124
GRIFFITH A. 134; Edward 103, 127, 203; George 132, 134, 136, 146, 164, 211; John 62; John L. 116; Luke 96; Mr. 133; Mrs. 192
GRINDAGE Eliza 59
GRINDAGER Eliza 36

GROOME Dr. 78, 84; Dr. John 32; Isaac P. 62; J. C. 10; John 15, 42; John C. 10; Major John R. 78
Grove Point 71
Grove, The 105
GRUBB Alex E. 92; Alexander 54; Alexander E. 23; Mrs. 1, 46
GRUPY Eliza B. 205; Jacob 205
Guffy's Delight 99
Guffy's Romantic Prospect 99
GURLIE Joseph 84
GUSTAVUS Frank 183
GUY Samuel Jr 87
GUYTON Edward M. 177, 195; James 100, 111, 183, 195; John 100; Joshua 98, 148, 191, 195; Joshua Jr 124; Priscilla 106
GYBSON Abraham 183

HACKETT James 102; Nicholas 124; William 11
HAGANY Rev J. 88
HAINES & GREER 35
HAINES Jacob 14; Job 35
HALE Colin F. 89
HALL & HUGGINS 18; 108
HALL Andrew 11; Ann 182; Ann Maria 56; Aquila 105, 182; Benedict 104; Benedict Edward 94; Capt Henry 96; Carvell 39; Charles G. 102, 130; Charles Penrose 198; Delia M. 138; Edward 96, 100, 104, 164; Frances 177; George W. 117; George Wiliam 140, 164, 211; Henry 94, 192; Isaac 28; J. C. C. 96; Maj. Henry 116; Manuel 53; Robert 56; Sidney 195; Thomas 6; W. T. 121; Walter T. 94, 96, 132, 138, 177, 192, 198; Washington 13, 23; William A. 87
Hall's mill 140
Hall's meadows 104
Hall's Purchase 192
HAMER William H. 6, 53, 60, 67
HAMILTON James 19
HAMMOND Nathan 127
HAMPHILL Andrew 134
HANNA Alexander 211. 118, 168, 185; Hannah 211; John 185; Mr. 131; Richard 46; William 107
HANNAH John 177; Sarah 88
HANNAWAY Thomas 177
HANSON Benedict 171; James 12; John 127, 136, 152; Joseph 11, 59
Hanson's Regnedged Neck 208

HANWAY Eliza 144; Joseph 137; Thomas 124; Washington 124; William 106
HAR... Abraham 95
Hard Bargain 176
HARDING P. 5, 15, 63; Sarah A. 34
HARDY George 35
Harford Republican and People's Advocate (Newspaper) 199
HARKINS Aaron 183; Hester 116; Joseph 133
HARLAN John 44; Joseph 14, 27, 84, 187; M. H. 44   169
HARLAND Hannah 106; Henry 111; Jerry 111
HARLI Hanna 195
HARLON Josephs 67
HARMAN Andrew 40
HARMER Abraham 111, 183; John 111, 174; Joseph 111; Joshua 111
Harmony Cotton Factory 3
HARPER Alexander 195; Caleb 15; Charles C. 108; Rev George S. 95; Samuel, Senr 167
HARRIS B. W. 61; Benjamin 103; Benjamin W. 6, 14, 39, 68, 87; Benoni 39; Catherine Marion 74; Charles 18, 87; George 111; John 59; John D. 169; Richard of Elisha 41; Sarah 74; Squire 29
HARRISON Thomas B. 172
HARROD William 133, 190
HARRY David 106, 169; Isaac 111; Joel 108, 111; Mary 95, 133, 183
HARSON Samuel 80
HART James 13; John T. 3; Joseph 124; Robert 87
HARTLEY Jesse 96
HARTSHORN S. 30
HARVEY James 102, 121, 209; John 133
HASSEN Mary 79
HASTINGS Henry 84, 92
HATCHKINS Rev H. N. 34
HAWKINS Abraham 59; Isaac 121, 172; Mary 96; Matthew 177; Mr.30; Robert 189
HAYES Henry 36; Henry M. 22; Samuel 87; Stephen 32
HAYS Archer 128, 161; Eleanor 25; N. 107, 116, 183; Robert H. 25; Susan 35, 43; T. A. 107, 116, 183; Thomas 195; Thomas A. 102, 132, 136, 161, 169, 175, 185, 189, 203; William 104; William S. 118
HAYWARD Thomas Jr 31

HAZLOP Benjamin W. 7
HEALEY James 111; John 111
HEAPS Archibald 111; Jane 159, 175; John 111, 177; Lloyd 111
HEATH Uptan S. 108
HEATON John 177
HENDERSON & BRYAN 59
HENDERSON A. F. 60; Andrew F. 11; F. 77; Frisby 8, 40, 44, 87; George 102, 183; James N. 183; John 40, 53, 124; Robert 132; Robert J. 195; Robert s. 177; Robert T. 124
HENDRICKS Hannah 92; Stephen 79
HENKLE Eli 146
HENLEY I. D. 98
HENNING John A. 134
HENRIS William 4
HENRY & BIDDLE 124
HENRY Isaac 102; Samuel 102, 164
HENSHAW J. 203; Rev 106
HEPHRON Joseph 84
HERBERT John 103, 207; Margaret 207; Phelix 111
HERDMAN Jefferson, M. D. 39; John 4, 58
Herman's Addition 101
HERNEY John 25
HERRIN Rev 179
HERRING Rev. 185
HERVEY James 183
HESSEY Henry 29
HESSON Francis Alison 91; William 34, 91
HEWITT William 15, 73, 87
HICKCOCK Asael 169
HICKS Elias 91; Jemima 91
HIGBEE Rev Daniel 91
HIGGINS Anthony 64; B. D. 134; Rev 76
HILDT George 134
HILES Nathan 91
HILLES Nathan 9
HILTON Miles 121, 133, 195
HINDS Alexander 59; Thomas 15
HINES Isaac 71
HINKLE Eli 143; Rev Eli 139
HIPKINS Caleb M. 137
Hisponilia 18
HITCHCOCK Amelia 104; Isaac 210
HOBBS Benjamin 127
HODGES James 44
HOGG Mr. 2; Samuel R. 8, 63; William 14, 87
HOGGSON Robert 59
HOKE Peter 139

HOLIDAY Urban 19
Holing Refuge 208
HOLLAND Aaron 169; Patrick 95; R. W. 95; Robert W. 115, 177; Samuel 35; William 169
HOLLINGSWORTH A. D. 88; Ann B. 25; Henry 3, 32, 39, 46, 50, 51, 56, 67, 81, 87, 88; J. 88; Jesse 212; L. 88; Mrs. A. B. 10; Nathaniel 106; Samuel 30; Samuel Jr 59, 86; William 88, 92
Hollingsworth old mill 32
HOLLIS Clark 106, 203; Richard F. 183
Holly Hill 208
HOLT Isaac 92; John Weston 59
HOOD William Jr 37
HOOPER Richard 183
HOOPES Amos 133
HOOPMAN Jacob 118, 132, 177, 189; Peter 118
HOOVER Jacob 187
HOPE Capt Thomas 187; James 170, 189; Thomas 124, 165, 172, 189, 191, 195, 196
HOPKINS Dr. 136; Dr. Wakeman B. 157; Dr. Thomas C. 201; Dr. W. B. 183; Ephraim 111; Henry 28; James L. 111; Johm 109, 111, 115, 132, 177, 199; Joseph 100, 111; Joseph E. 111; Joseph K. 181; Joshua 111; Levin 111; Samuel 111; 205; William 111
HOPMAN Jacob 178; Peter 178
HORSEY Auterbridge 79; O. 29, 73
HOSKINS Cheyney 195
HOSSINGER Joseph 60
HOUCK Andrew 53
HOW James 111; John 111; William jun. 111; William, sen 111
HOWARD Benjamin C.108; Col. Edward A. 124, 171; Corelia 173; George R. 14, 84, 87; Joseph 137; Leonard 141; Mary 64; Peter 59; Rachel 63; Spencer 88; Thomas 4, 8, 14, 16; Thomas G. 132, 177; Thomas Gassaway 187; Thomas Jr 29. 74, 90; Thomas sen 16; William 4, 63
HUBART James 92
HUDSON James 34; Joshua S. 11; Sarah 57
HUFF Jesse 111; John 53; 183; Michael 111, 133; Thomas 111
HUGG Abm sen. 95; H. 68
HUGGINS James 133, 169; Thomas 5, 10

HUGHES Elizabeth 105; Everett S. 177; James 117, 118, 143, 162, 191; John T. 95; Mary L. 124; Samuel 98, 127
Hughs Samuel 59
HUGO Dr. Samuel B. 108; Samuel B. 108, 137
HUING Rev 206
HULL William C. 40
HURLOCK John 7
HUSBAND Herman 92; John 180; Joseph 194; Joshua 180, 189
Husband's Mill 4
HUTCHESON George 15; William 15
HUTCHINS Elizabeth 125; Thomas 191; William 125
Hutchinson's Meadows 99
HUTCHISON Sarah 79
HUTTON William 54
HUXULIS Sarah 15
HYATT Clark 96
HYLAMAN Howard 28
HYLAND Benjamin 15; Elizabeth 25; Jacob 25; John of Jacob 40; Joshua 71; Lambert G. 15; Major Nicholas 86, 88; Nicholas 7, 17, 36; Nicholas of Edward 11, 88; Ruth 88; Stephen 40
HYNSON Thomas B. 62

Improved Adventure, The 203
INGRAM John 111
Innkeeper Kenedy 30
IRELAND Joseph Jr 44
IRWIN Mr. 30; Samuel 15
Isaac's Enlargment 176
Islington 208

Jack's Purchase 203
JACKSON Ann C. 15; James 23, 32; President 135, 138, 199, 205; William N. 80
JAMAR Henry 13, 69. 84
James Hugh 54; Margaret 48; Mary 179; Rebecca 124; Samuel 106, 116, 194; Sarah 143, 169; Sedgwick 102, 143, 169
James Run Woollen manufactory 105
JAMESON George Jr 34
JANNEY Eli 11; James 14; John 1; Thomas 14, 28
JANNINGS John 11
JARRAT Abraham 101
JARRET Jesse 103
JARRETT A. 96; A. L. 5, 175; Abraham 94, 103. 104, 165, 170, 175, 195;

Amanda C. 175; Jesse 104; Jesse 191;
Luther 177; Luther M. 179
JARVIS Francis 92
JEFFERY James 202; Thomas 107, 204;
Thomas, Jr 133; Vincent 145
JENKINS Mary Ann 195; Moses 189
JENKS William D. 9, 16
JENNESS John 79
JENNINGS Rev 128
JERRETT Abraham 146
JERVIS John 135, 185
JESTER Outen 57
JEWETT John 5; John Jr 195
JOANS Joseph 116
JOB Daniel 8' Jacob 100, 172
JOBS Eliza 59
John & Mary's Highland 82
JOHNS Charles 7; H. 124; H. H. 133;
Henry 183; Henry H. 95, 100, 169, 195;
Kensey Jun 91; Mr. 137
JOHNSON ___ 95; A.C. 183; Ann 209;
C. D. W. 106, 108, 133, 183; Capt
207;Capt C. D. W. 124; Catharine 80;
Charles 183; Charles D. W. 126, 132,
150; Dr. Caleb M. 169; Dr. James 116;
Elisha 111; James 53, 82, 111; James,
M.D. 161; Jane 95, 124; John 94, 101,
105, 203, 211; John L. 125, 180; John
M. 32; Josiah 106, 111, 132, 133, 195;
Margarett 183; Mrs. 133; Mrs. Sane
133; Reverdy 108; Robert 92; Samuel A.
106; Sarah 124; Susan Ann of Thomas
183; Thomas 96. 111, 147, 183; William
M. 180
Johnson's mill 105
JOHNSTON Jacob 14, 39; James 57; John
M. 22, 68; Joshua 25; Robert 84
Johnston's Choice 99
JOLLY John 121; William 121; William
D. 159
JONES Amos 111, 129; Aquila 209; B.
G. 95; Benedict 59, 87; Benj. G. 183;
Benjamin G. 106, 126, 133; Cadwalader
172; Christopher 29; Daniel 180;
Deborah 34; Elias 111; Elijah 111;
Eliza 62; Elizabeth 206; Ellis 76;
George 31, 32, 35, 83, 84; Gilbert
175; Henry H. 116; Hezekiah 29; Hugh
111; James 51, 98, 111, 195; John 22,
111; Joseph 98, 111; L. Cadwalader
209; Lemen 111; Maria 86; Mary 180;
Mary A. 116; Mr. S. 106; Owen C. 55;
Rebecca 83; Reubin 98; Robert 53;
Sarah 22, 62; Stephen 116, 124. 132.

133. 177, 190, 195, 211; Theophilus
183, 195; Thomas 7, 86; William 16, 66
Jones Inheritance 118, 165
Jones Zackeus 58
Jones' Venture 100
Jonns H. H. 180
JORDAN John 111, 195; Robert H. 134
JORDON John 15, 87
JOURDEN Wiliam 133
JUDD John 171, 195

KAAS Charles 59
KAIN Thomas 133
KALBFUS Charles 134
KARR George H. 43; Samuel 43
KARSNER George 59
KAWKY Kolan 79
KEAN James 103; John 2, 39. 63, 67.
116. 161, 165, 169, 170; John 177;
Mathew 4; Matthew 54; Richard H. 133;
Timothy 132
KEASBY Edward S. 34, 77
KEECH Rev 144, 148, 176; Rev J. R.
211; Rev John R. 95, 131, 138, 180,
205
KEEN Timothy 97, 177
KEERENS Levi 96
KEETLY Richard 72
KELL T. 150; Thomas 137, 143
KELLEY James 98
KELLY Thomas 106, 108, 177; William
124
KENDRICK Daniel 65
KENEDY James, Junr 116; Joseph 169
KENNADY William 111
KENNARD Dr. Thomas C. 62; Matthew 106,
183; Thomas 89; William H. 95
KENNEDY Elihu B. 103; James 103, 105;
John P. 108; Joseph 177; William 102
KENNEY William 195
KEPER Samuel 134
KERR Alexander 103, 111; Alexander M.
95; Charlotte 60; Edward 111, 124,
127, 132, 166; Elizabeth 92, 179;
George H. 6; Mary 195; Robert 3, 39,
44, 111' Samuel 2, 3, 39, 40, 44, 47,
51, 65; William 95, 103
KESLEY Rev William 194; William 194
KEVENEUGH Lag 80
KEYSER Samuel 98
KID John Taylor 127
KIDD ___ 52; George 7, 36; James 160;
Jane 3, 46; Joshua 160; Penelia 160
Kidd's Troubles 160

KILEN Henry 36
KILGORE Ann R. 36; William 40, 41, 53
KILGOUR James 87
KIMBLE & DUNCAN 97
KIMBLE Hiram 30
KINADE Samuel 111
KING Abraham 105; Abram 131; Elizabeth Ann 131; John 35; Lewis 175
King's Tavern 155
KINKEAD Alexander 87; William 60
KINSEY ___ 52
Kinsley Reads' Addition 52
KIRK Amelia 79; Benjamin C. 61; E. 37; Elisha 14, 37, 68; John 177; Timothy 37; William 46
KIRKWOOD Jabez 95, 124; William C. 195
KITCHEN Peter 97
KIZER David 98
KNIGHT Aquila 186; George 28; Immer 14; James 51, 98, 115, 192; Robert 65; Thomas 194
KNITZBURY Elizabeth 29
KNOCK Ann 71; Benjamin 39, 43, 57
KROUSS Leonard 17

LA RUE Elizabeth 183
LACKEY John M. 79
LAIRE Thomas 79
LAMBERT Gersham W. 7
LAMBORN Eli 63
LAMBURN Daniel 105; John S. 105
LANCASTER Hester 136; Martha 195
LANGDON Aberilla M. 183; Richard C. 161, 189
LANSDALE Mary M. 195; William M. 128
LAWLIS John D. 30
LAWRENCE William 201
LEAKE Jesse 116
LEAKIN Sheppard C. 198
LEARNED J. D. 164; L. D. 108
LEARY George 144
LeBARON Dr. Francis 28
LECOUNT Mr. 13
LEE Capt 39; Charles sen 111; Ellen 29; James 111; John 95; Mary 150, 171; Parker H. 142, 150; Parker Hall 175; Richard D. 141, 177, 181; Samuel 111; Samuel W. 171; Samuel Worthington 175; Sarah 10; William 71, 92; William D. 109, 119, 121
Lee's Mill 115
LEECH Rev John R. 110
Legoe's Point 209
Legs and Arms 102

Leigh of Leighton 191
LEILSON John M. 116
LEMMON George 116
LEMON Sarah 205
LENNEN Ann 183
LEPENETTE Rev M. 92
LESTER Mary 179; William 99, 179
LEVERING Enoch 19; Jesse 19
LEWIS Elizabeth 183; Jacob 97; John 177; Philip 25; Sarah 15
Liberty Mills 126
LIGGIT William 210
LIGHTNER George W. 87
LILLY John 189; Thomas 106
LINDENBERGER George 100; Jacob 100
LINDSAY William 177
LINDSEY Eliza 137; John 72; Susan 91; William 102
LINGUM John 116
Lion Tents 181
LITLE E. 116
LITTLE Anglesea 40; Ann 92; Christopher 6, 52; Col. 147; Elizabeth 95; Mary 52
Little Britain 54, 69
Littlejohn's tavern 144
LLOYD Evan 190
LOCKWOOD Richard 35
Locust Point 83
Lofflin's Neglect 98
LOFLIN Mary 200; Mr 204; Mrs. 204; William 200
LOGAN Mary 108; Robert 5
LOGUE James 179; William 202
LONG Daniel 116, 195; Hr. 116; James 34
LONGFELLOW David R. 85; Gideon 85
LOOCKERMAN Thomas W. 91
LORT Joseph 53
LOVE Bennet 115, 176, 185; John 101, 127, 177; Robert 3, 4, 46; Samuel 59; William 95
LOVETT Margareta 56
LOWE Joshua 46; Thomas 37
LUCKEY James 132
LUDENUM John 25
LUFFBOROUGH Nathan 98
LUKENS Benjamin 124
LUNN John 39
LUSBY Eleanor 37; Elizabeth 5; Mr. 2, 66; R. C. 9, 69, 91; Robert C. 5, 6, 57, 65, 71, 90; Zebulon 29
LYARSON Andrew 15
LYERSON Elizabeth 79

LYNCH   P. L. 92; Peregrine L. 87
LYON John C. 134; Mr. 50
LYONS Robert 106
LYTLE Charles 111; Ephraim 118; James 116, 132, 177; James Jr 148, 169

M'...MEDTY John 95
M'ADOW Andrew 106
M'ATEE Francis   111; Henry 170
M'CABE James 53
M'CAREY John 95
M'CARNAN John 95
M'CARTNEY Edward 130
M'CASLIN Ann 15
M'CAULEY Daniel 10; Margaret 92
M'Clarrys Mrs.44
M'CLASKEY Ellis 96; James 115, 180
M'CLAY William 10
M'CLELLAN Hetty 45
M'CLINTON John 59
M'CLUER Isaiah 59
M'CLURE German 84
M'COCKLE John 3
M'COLLOUGH John 31
M'COMAS James S. 132, 177; Preston 99
M'CONCHEY ___ 52
M'CORD John 1, 2, 15, 50, 54
M'CORKLE John 35, 82, 87
M'CORMICK Ann 25
M'COWELL James 3
M'COY Charles 34; Joseph 22, 111; William, jun 111
M'CREERY Samuel 53
M'CRERY Thomas 28
M'CULLOUGH Samuel 5; William 54
M'CUMMINGS William 59
M'CUMMINS William 36
M'CUTCHEN John D. 11
M'DONALD George 53; John 53
M'DOWELL James C. 1, 46, 65
M'ELEARYS Mrs. 3
M'ELLARY Eliza 82
M'FADDON Thomas 111
M'GAW James 132
M'GAY Samuel 211
M'GINNIS Catharine 51; Hugh 51
M'GOMERY Robert 111;Thomas 111
M'GREGOR James 36
M'ILVAIN John 46
M'INTIRE Andrew 56; 83; Samuel 8
M'JILTON William 111
M'KAIGE John 53
M'KENNEY John 181; John Jr 194; John Jr, P.M. 95; John, Jr 114

M'KENN John 111
M'KENSEY Zebulon 28
M'KINLEY Margaret 15
M'KINSEY Benjamin 53; Susan 66
M'LAUGHLIN Matthew 52
M'NABB James 111; John 106; William 111
M'NUTT William 111
M'VEY Henry 86
M'WEEN James 36
MACATEE George 176; Henry 97, 102, 176; Samuel 176
MACAULY Patrick 108
MACKALL Benjamin F. 11, 14, 32, 59, 86; Henry F. 29
MACKEY Anne 46; Catherine 46; David 6, 34, 65, 79; Jacob 15; John 28, 87; Mary 124; William 12, 18, 27, 28, 87
MACKLAN Ann 88
MACLAY William 11
MADDEN John F. 177
MAFFIT John W. 30
Maffit's Mill 30
MAGAW James 24; Rev James 21
MAGNESS Benjamin 197; James 195; John 133, 169; Sarah Eliza 197; William sr 177
MAGRAW James 37; Rev 45, 80; Rev James 66
MAGREDY Mr. D. 14
MAHAN George 39; Reece 53; William 84
MAHON James 117; Sarah 117
MAHR David 35
Maiden's Mount 98
MALOME John 92
MALONE Bernard 96
MALSBY David Lee 177; David sen 105; Morris 116, 133, 201, 208
MANLEY Sarah 5; William 5
MANLOVE John 11; John S. 79
MANLY Charles K. 34; John 41; Mr. 14
MANSFIELD Catharine Ann 10
MAREAN Silas 208
MARKLAND E. J., P.M. 207; Edward J. 78, 111, 125, 177; Edward J., P.M. 194
MARLEY James 92
MARNES Samuel 27, 84
MARPPONGEN William 79
MARSELL John 92
MARSH Dr. Benjamin 96
MARSHAL William 101
MARSHALL Ann M. 183; John 14, 15, 34, 68, 87; Stewart 116, 183
Marshall's tavern 147

MARSHAND(?) John 195
MARTIN Abraham 139; James 28; Mary 183; Michael 65
Martin Rev Dr.179
Martin's Ludgate 98
Mary's Lot 97, 127, 143
MASON Ann 116; Mary A. 169
MASSEY Aquila 111; Isaac 111; James 78; Joshua W. 81; Louisa 84; Major J. 84; Nicholas 43; Rigba 111
MATHER James 109
MATHEWS James 28, 32, 38; Jon 53; Josiah 164; Lloyd 164
Mathews' Enlargement 99
MATLACK Jonathan 103
Matthew's Enlargement 141
MATTHEWS John C. 204; Mary 204; William 6
MAULDEN John 87
MAULDIN John 11
MAULSBY Colonel I. D. 187; David 124, 185; David J. 183; I. 195; I. D. 150, 155, 172, 196, 208; Midshipman J. H. 124
MAXWELL Robert 54; William 53
MAYNADIER Henry G. 133, 183
MCANN Charles 183
MCATEE Cloe 195; Henry 177; Silvester 183
MCBLAIN ___ 133
MCCALLA William 79
MCCAULEY John 79
MCCAUSLAND Jefferson 132; Robert 137, 177
MCCLASKEYJames 187
MCCLEARY Ephraim 195
McCleery's Half Purchase 173
MCCLURE German 195; Thomas 133
MCCLUSKEY Mr. 209
MCCOMAS Alexander, Jr 176; Amos 183, 195; Charles 102. 143; Joshua Jr 102
MCCOMASS John 183
MCCONKEY James 140
MCCONNELL James 137, 183
MCCORKLE John 91
MCCOWN Hugh 133, 159
MCCOY William 111
MCCRACKEN Sarah 183, 195
MCCREA Robert 116
MCCREADY Thomas 12
MCCREERY Elizabeth 32; Jesse 32; Thomas 32; William 32
MCCRODAN James 167, 169

MCCULLOUGH John 87; Catharine 172; George 183
MCDANIEL William 91
MCDONNEL Patrick 202
MCELDERRY Ann 187; Hugh 108, 127; Thomas 187
MCFADDEN Elizabeth 121, 124; James 124; John 104, 121; John B. 118
MCFADDON John B. 183
MCGAW James 127, 175, 177; John of Robert 133; Samuel 133
MCGAY Samuel 183
MCGEE Rev 173; Rev Thomas 171; Thomas 134, 143
MCGLAUGHLIN George 169
MCGOLDRICK Patrick 82
MCJILTON Frances C. 177; William 127, 207
MCKENNEY J. 131; John 132; John Jr 106, 135, 159; John Jr, P.M. 106, 124, 116, 133
MCKINLEY Patrick 103
MCKOWAN Samuel 31
MCLAUGHLIN Ann 190; David 127; Frances 195; George 190; John 190; Nancy 190; Robert 190; Samuel 190
MCMATH Mary 148
MCNEIL Francis A. 134
MCVEY Elder 129; Henry 91; James 124, 190
MEAD James 183
MEADE James 195
MEADS Elisha 191; James 191
MEARNS Abel 19
Measles outbreak 140
MECHEM Dr. 135
MEDFORD Eliza L. 62
MEGINNISS C. 51;Mary 51
MEGREDY John 86
MENDENHALL Joseph 13, 68
MERCER Ann 29; Benjamin 29; James 34; William D. 30, 38, 77
MERKEL William 39
MERKLE William 39
Merrikens Inheritance Forever 136
METEER Samuel 30; William 30
MICHAEL Col. 134; Col. Jacob 185; Daniel 185; Ethan 190; Jacob 97, 109, 115, 121, 132, 151, 177; Levinia 125; Mr. 105; William 106, 116, 134, 183, 185, 195
Michaelsville 115, 121
MICHEL Capt R. 25
MILBURN Margaret 34

MILES Aquila 114; Capt James 54; Francesina 53; Joseph, Jr 121; Mr. 147; Thomas 191
Militia meetings, drills and parades 67, 102, 109. 110, 149, 191; court martial 187
Mill Privilege 4
MILLER Adeline F. 110; Albert 62; Andrew 183, 195; Augustus 25, 53; Charles 7; David 29; Deborah 4; Dr. William 28; Henry D. 57; Horatio 111; Jacob 159; James 4, 96; James M. 154; John 36; John M. 4; Joseph A. 36; Joseph W. 9, 28; Lewis 88; Louis 50; Maria 62; Mary 28; Rev Thomas 92; Samuel 4, 7, 8, 35, 81, 85; Solomon 30; Thomas 11; Thomas Jr 17, 69, 92; William 9, 35, 42, 111, 159; William C. 4, 49; William F. 104, 107, 114, 158; William jr. 1
MILLES Joseph 28
Mills; of Aquilla Hall 140; Back Creek Mills 73; Cecil Mills 182; Cranberry Mill 130; Davis' Saw Mill 201; on Deer Creek 136; Fisher's Mill 4; Gilpin's Mill 84; Gover's Mill 185; Hollingsworth's old mill 32; Husband's mill 4; of Jacob Hoopman 189; Johnson's mill 105; Lee's Mill 115; Liberty Mills 126; at Morgan's Creek (described) 12; of Nathan S. Bemis 149; Paper mills 25; Parker's mill 134, 202; Patterson's Mill 198; Philips Mill 31; Porter's mill 44; Preston's Mill 135; Stafford Mills 102; Yellot's Mill 105;
Mine Bank 170
MINER Thomas 31
MINNICK Jacob 133
MITCHEL Col. 147; Richard 117, 118
MITCHELL A. D. 34; Abarilla 161; Abraham D. 28
Mitchell Capt 33; Charles 118; Dr. George E. 154; Edward 161, 186, 1891; Gerard 130; Jacob 137; James 87; James G. 116; James W. 169; John 131; John A. 183; Kent 100, 187; Lydia 186; Mary Ann 157; Richard 191
MITON Job 195
MITTAN John 29
MITTON Job 133, 183
MOFFITT John S. 87
MOHLEN Jacob J. 157
MONAMIS John 96

MONEY C. C. 91
MONK Minerva 169
MONKS Francis E. 132; William 170
MONTGOMERY Dr. James 106; 124; 142; 195; 197; Jehu 172; Michael 51; Thomas 1, 51, 124; William B. 106
MOODY Samuel 183, 195
MOOR George 96
MOORE Amos 53; Capt J. 25; D. L. 28; Elijah 79; George 6, 157; James G. 34, 72; Jane 15; Jason 94f, 103, 126. 132, 186. 203; John 53, 62; Joseph 95, 183; Lucretia G. 195; Martha 37; Mary 6; Moses 14; Parker 104; Philip 142; Robert 36; Stephen 29; Thomas 14, 87
MOORES James 108, 118, 119, 121, 132, 148, 194; P. 106
MORE Joseph 111
MORGAN Hamilton 177; Hannah 96, 202; James 1; James Jr 40; John L. 79; Lorenza D. 16; Maj. Robert 111; Robert 98, 121; Thomas 34; William 11
Morgan's Creek 12
MORRIS Hannah 106; Sarah 106
MORRISON Ambrose 111; David 106, 133; Ezekiel 209; Hannah 124; John 111. 195; Mathew 111; Peter V. 177; Rev 124, 171
MORROW James 32, 34, 90; James H. 53
MORTON John B. 87
Mount Ararat 56
Mount Friendship 146, 175
Mount Friendship Farm 175
Mount Pleasant 198
Mount Vernon 97, 114, 118
MOUNT William C. 42
Mountain Farm 5
Mulberry Point 94
MULFORD T. 13, 68
MULLEN Barney 19; Elizabeth 19; William 29, 37, 84
MULLIGEUR Abraham 183
MULLIN Barny 31; Elizabeth 31
MULLIT Thomas 15
MULOW John S. 34
MUNNIKHUYSEN Dr. 181; J. H. 124; Jacob H. 145, 190; John H. 166; Mr. 186
MUNROE Jonathan 134
MURDOCK Catharine 34
MURPHEY John 102; John C. 29
MURPHY Capt 96, 192; Elizabeth 28; John C. 29
MURRAY Elizabeth 101
MUSGRAVE J. 15

Negro Swamp Fishery 88
Neighbours' Good Will 181
NELSON Aquila 97; James 154, 160, 195; John 94; William 106, 185
NESBIT S. Jr, P.M. 80
NESBITT S. 25; S. Jr, P.M. 30; Samuel Jr 16, 94
New Garden 18
New Hall 17, 40
New Marshal 39
New Munster 23
NEWELL Sarah 103
NEWLAND Charles A. 11
NEWLIN David 106, 169, 201; Rebecca 169
NEWTON Basil 145
NIAK T. H. 195
NIBLOCK William 49
NICHOLS Sarah Ann 88
NICHOLSON John 136; William 15
NICKLE Archibald 36
NISBIT M. 30
NIVIN David 41; Tabitha 41
NORMAN Henry 15, 25
NORRINGTON Sarah 116
NORRIS Alexander 124, 169, 194; Aquila 208; Capt 172; D. 183; David 169; Dr. 103; Edward of Edward 177; Isaac 183, 195; John 99, 132, 139, 157, 159, 161; John C. 132, 171, 177, 195, 204; Lloyd M. 90; Luther A. 124, 159, 165, 203, 208; Mary 161, 208; Rhesa 132, 146; Vincent 106, 124, 132, 177, 195
NORTON Thomas 95
NOTTINGHAM West 135
NOWLAND Alfred 68; Alfred C. 14; Edward 150; Eliza 150; Elizabeth 57; Mary 18; Maria 150; Matilda 150; Peregrine 150, 186; Rebecca 99, 150; Sophia 150
NUGENT Sylvester 15, 34

O'BRIEN Rev 175, 176; Rev T. 106; Rev Timothy 84
O'CONNOR James 144
Obadiah's Venture 203
Old Man's Meadows 127
OLDHAM Charles 4, 15, 28, 40, 53, 89; Cyrus 6, 14, 27, 34, 87; Edward 34; Edward jr 3, 40; Emily 15; George W. 41; Maria 53, 79; Mary A. 36; Samuel 43
Onions Meadow Ground 99

ORR Thomas 42; William 13, 36, 42, 57, 87
Orr's Survey 173
OSBORN Harriet 151; William 169
OSBORNE Amos 177; Aquila 118
OUTTIN William H. 80
OWENS Francis 6; Mrs. 31; Pollard 7; Richard 101; Thomas 79

PACA William 99
Paca's Enlargement 190
PAINER Benjamin of Benjamin 177
PANNEL James 177
PANNELL James 169, 185
Paper mills 25
PARIOT Ruth 179
PARK Rev 125, 159, 176, 181
PARKE Rev 131, 173, 178, 179, 201, 209
PARKER Caleb 7, 71; Dr. 66; James 92; Joseph 111, 135; Robert 111, 177; Robert, jr 169; Thomas 15
Parker's Folly 208
Parker's Mill 134, 202
PARKINSON Samuel 133, 195
PARSONS Joseph 62
Partnership Dissolved 170
PARTRIDGE John 5, 34, 82; Joseph G. 14, 42, 67
PASCHELL Stephen 32
PASQUET William H. 185
PATTERSON Aaron 128; Hannah 133; Henry 50; Jane 1; John 3, 7, 39; Thomas 96; William 1, 97
Patterson's Field 109
Patterson's Mill 198
Patterson's Old Fields 191
PAUL James 164; Thomas 164
Peach bottom 140
PEACOCK George 63, 40, 88; Mr. 2, 25, 32; Thomas 7, 91
PEARCE Benjamin 18, 51; Davidson D. 7, 22; Edward 78; Elizabeth 2, 51; Matthew 15; William R. 18
Pearce's Neck 18
Pearce's Tavern 51
Pearch Creek 75
Pearson's Pen 191
Pearson's Range 167, 187
PECKARD Henry L. 83
PENDLETON Daniel 98
PENINGTON Azarias 11; Elias 11; Robert 71; William C. 36
PENNIMAN Thomas 138

PENNINGTON Abraham F. 87; Benedict 82; Edward 31; Elias 87, 92; George 79 Hyland 61; John H. 8; Mary 92; William 53, 59
PEREMAN George 183
PERREY Ellen 52
PERRY John 94
PERRYMAN Caroline E. 195; Isaac 134, 211
PERYMAN Ann 183
Philip's Mills 31
PHILIPS John sen 36; Mr. 30
PHILLIPS James Senr 129; Joseph 59; Martha 129; Nancy 53; Samuel 37
PHYSIC Adriana 30
PHYSICK Edmund 3, 16, 17, 25, 30; Elizabeth 30; Henry W. 17
PIERCE William 87
PINER William 36
PITCOCK Benjamin 177
Planter's Neglect 208
Pleasant Hills 103
Pleasant Plains 102
Plough, the 98
Plumb Point 7, 71
Plumb Point Farm 64
PLUMLY George 124
POAG John 32; Martha 32; Samuel 32
POISAL John 134; 179
POLHAMUS Thomas 59
POLK William 18
POPE Folger 111, 116
Poplar Neck 66
PORTER Andrew Jr 102; Andrew R. 1, 35, 46; David 92; Eleanor 35; Hugh 150; James 192; John H. 11; Mary 34
Porter's and Grubb's Folly 65
Porter's mill 44
POTEE Francis 195
POTEET Poteet 182; Corbin 177; James 133; Rev 172, 179; Thomas 95
Preistford 121, 123
PRESBURY George of William 192; George William 187; William R. 187
PRESTON Avarilla J. 116; D. H. 169; Dr. A. 195; Dr. Alonzo 91; Dr. Jacob A. 108; Eliza Ann 183; Isaac 195; Jacob A. 136, 159; James B. 105; James Bond 132; Jonas 3; Mrs. E. A. 124; Rachel 116; Sarah 106; Scott 183; William 3, 46
Preston's Mill 135
PRETTYMAN William 134
PREVAIL John 111

PRIBE Jacob 92
PRICE Ambrose 1, 35, 43; Ambrose M. 8; Ann 15; Anne 9; Benjamin 5. 50; Catharine 9, 43, 53, 59; Elizabeth H. 89; Fredus 5, 19, 31; George 33; Hugh 27; Hyland 19, 27, 41, 48; Isaac 18; Jacob 84, 87; James Hyland 27; Jane 212; John 27; John B. 9; John Boyer 43; John C. 48; John H. 29, 150, 155, 164, 195; John R. 71; John V. 11, 28, 30; Lilburn 12, 29; Louis 5, 89; M. H. 133; Mrs. E. H. 29; Samuel 36; William 9, 96, 177
PRICHETT Mr. 195
Priest's Ford 99
PRIGG Dr. Joseph 110; Edward 116; Edward of William 177; Parker 111; William 175; William T. 71
PRIMROSE Reuben H. 46
PROCTER William G. 116
PROCTOR Thomas 111; William G. 124
Prospect Hill 4, 63, 64
PRYCE Mary W. 76; O. C. 15
PRYOR Thomas 14
PUE Caleb 180
PUGH ___ 52; Ann 46; Humphrey 46; James 8, 34; Lewis 60
PURDEE Rev Isaac 81
PURNELL Bennett 48; Caroline 59; Elizabeth A. 56; Greenbury 56; James 37, 87; Miss C. 92; Samuel T. 37
PURVES Adam 65
PYLE Amos 104; Daniel 104; David 111, 183; Isaac Junr 195; John 104; Joseph 104; Lewis 209; Lewis T. 194; Mary 201; Nathan 111; Orphia 104; Phebe 104; Richard 196; Ruth 104; Samuel 104; William 129, 183, 202
Pyle's Saw Mill 129

QUALLS John 111
QUIGLEY Hugh 111
QUIMBY Elizabeth 33
QUINLAN Charity 84

RADCLIFFE William 15
RAILY and MIDDLEBOROUGH 147
RAITT John 90
RAMPLEY James 124
RAMSAY Samuel 87; Thomas 58; William W. 32, 168
RAMSEY Andrew 1; Daniel 23; Henry C. 5; James 59; Samuel 1; William W. 61
RANDALL Beale 108

RAPHEL Mrs. E. 169
RARICK John 84
RARRICK John 32
RASIN Phillip 76
RATLIFF Margaret 9
RAWLING John 46
RAWLINGS John 11, 87, 92
RAWLINS John 73, 87
RAY James 31
RAYMOND Daniel 176
READ Andrew 52; John 52; William 52
REARDAN James 99, 101
REASON Jane 33; John Washington 33
REDDEN Andrew 105
REDGRAVES Mary 60; William M. 60
REDUE Joseph 11; Joseph, P.M. 62
REED Brig. Gen. Philip 160; Joseph 36; Mary 84; Rev 167; Samuel 132, 160, 177, 190; Thomas 46, 53, 183
REESE Ann 195
RELEA William 59
RENSHAW John 133; Joseph 132; Ruth 133
REXFORD Samuel 25
REYNOLDS David 39; Henry 28; Isaac 13; Israel 5, 10, 89; Joel 1; John 19; Joseph 79; Mary 28; Richard 1; S., jr 30; Taylor 87; Thomas 87; William 22
RHODES Z. 198
RICE Washington 28
RICH Level 101
RICHARDSON Benjamin 115, 132, 146, 177; Elry 46; Henrietta 183; Isaac 135; J. 74; Joseph 5; Joshua 8, 14, 46; Major William 190; Thomas T. 195; Maj. William 124, 187; Margaret 106; Mintus 53; Morgan 171; Mrs. Richard 124; R. 134; R... 95; Rev 166, 177, 197; Rev Benjamin 136; Robert 104, 132, 177, 183; Samuel 178; Samuel M. 168; Vincent 169, 183, 195; William 15, 94, 102, 105, 120, 132, 135, 171
RICKETS David 10; William 10
RICKETTS George 64; Nathan 103; Rachel 22, 68; Thomas M. 177; William 25, 32, 34, 37
Ricketts' Triangle 17
RIDDLE James 63; John 182
RIDER ___ 124; George 105, 116; James 15; James D. 28
RIDGELY Charles (governor) 144
RIELY William D. 79
RIGDAN Benjamin jr 111

RIGDON Alexander 111, 130; Benjamin 99, 111, 130; Elizabeth 130; George 111; William 111, 124
RILEY James 134, 207
RINGGOLD Edward 105
RIRACK John 92
RISTER George 183
RITCHERDSON Philip 133
ROACH H. 28; Howard 28; Thomas 31
ROBB Rev john 124
ROBBIN Charles 62
ROBERT John 53; Mary 29
Robert's Lot 101, 127
ROBERTS Capt William 66
ROBERTSON Graftin 111; Isaac 133; John 111
ROBESON Elizabeth 23
Robinhood's Forest 127
ROBINSON Charles 191; Ephraim 15; Grace 28; Isaac 183, 195; John 107, 135, 183; John, P.M. 169, 195; Joseph 177; Mary 36; William 34, 84
ROBISON William 53
ROCHESTER & HOWARD 38
ROCHESTER Martha 88; William 14, 33, 34, 53
ROCKHOLD Francis 104; Jesse 124; John 94, 95, 104
ROCKLAND Estate 25
RODENHISER Peter 103; Phillip 140
RODGERS John 195; Rowland 177
RODMAN Mary 83; Philip 83
ROGERS Esther 106; James 95; John 51, 116, 169; Joseph 111; Rowland 116, 133; Samuel 111; Thomas 51
Rogers' Mill 13, 31
ROLAND Samuel 40
ROSS & WILEY 89
ROSS John 12, 87, 92
ROSSEL Mary 15
ROWE Thomas 15
ROWLAND James 87; Samuel 1
RUAN Dr. 39; John G. 10
RUDOLPH Michael 39; Miss H. D. 34; Tobias 36
RUDULPH & TORBERT 33
RUDULPH Maria 86; Tobias 9, 15, 22, 59, 86; Zeb 10, 41, 52, 84; Zebulon 11, 91
RUFF Capt Henry P. 196; Hannah 124; Henry 95; Henry P. 104, 177, 203
RULY Samuel 18
Rumney Marsh 106, 152
RUMSEY John 98

RUSH Ester 95
RUSSEL James 103; Rev A. K. 60, 91
Russel's Chance 127
RUSSELL Thomas 31, 33
RUTLEDGE Capt 149; Edward 177; Elisha 129, 133; Ignatius 111; Jane W. 124; John W. 132, 160, 177, 195; Joshua 95, 185, 195; Mary 95; William 133, 169
RUTTER Thomas 46
RYAN John F. 87
RYDER Rev William 74, 118; William 71
RYLAND Joseph P. 43, 79

SALISBURY James 3, 46
SAMPLE John 98; Samuel C. 53
SANDERS George 87; Joseph 175; Margaret 175
SANKS James 134
SAPPINGTON Dr. John 111, 121, 177; Jarrad 183; John, M. D. 105; Thomas 183; William 117, 118, 187
SAULSBURY Mary 59
Saulsbury Plains 173
SAUNDERS John 118, 165; Joseph 126; Margaret 118; Mary 118; Robert 118, 170; Robert Banker 118; William 118
SAVIN Thomas L. 11, 49; William F. 90
SAWYER William 124
SCAFF John 169
SCARBOROUGH Charles 92; John 92; Watson 34
SCARBROUGH Archibald 111; Benjamin 111; James 111; John 111; Samuel 95, 111
SCARBUROUGH John 94
SCARF Henry 95, 116; John 195
SCARFF Henry 160; James 160; John 202; Joshua 160; Julia Ann 160, 179
SCHAEFFER F. George 46
SCOLEY Reuben 62
SCOTT Alexander 2, 4, 8, 77, 88; Dr. Edward 42; Dr. J. H. 68; Hannah A. 195; J. H. 16; James 34, 36, 40; John 196; Joseph 96; Mary 42, 58, 163; Misses 127; Moses 5; Moses sen 58; Thomas 124; Mr. 105; Otho 97, 104, 133, 161, 169, 183, 191, 194, 195, 196; Thomas 58; William C. 25
SEAVILL Isaac 53
SENNEY George 30
SERGEANT Mr. 5
SERGANT Robert 15, 34, 53
SEVERSON Hance 2; John 31; Samuel 31; Thomas 31

SEVIN Ann 41; Margaret 41
SEWAL James 37
SEWALL & RICKETS 40
SEWALL Charles S. 171; Col. James 88; James 3, 5, 8, 11, 46, 67, 84, 86, 88
SEWELL Charles S. 169, 172, 187, 195; Rev Thomas 65
SHAFFER --- 16
Shamokin P. E. 134
Shandy Hall 192
SHARPLEY Mr 48
SHARP Aceniah 81; David S. 15; John 195; William 36
SHARPE Solomon, M.D. 74
SHARPLEY John 14; Rev John 42, 67
SHAW Elizabeth 160; William G. 145
SHEARER David 23; James 23; Jane 36
SHECKLE William 132
SHEED Margaret 116
SHEPHARD Jacob R. 134; John 61
Sheppard's Good Friendship 164, 169
SHERDIN James 116
SHERDING Ellen 133
SHEREDINE Ann 23; Daniel 49
SHERER Jane 79; John 79; W. 61
SHERIDINE Daniel 44, 46; James 124
SHERLACK John 79
SHERMIZER Jacob 58
SHIELDS Sarah 28
SHIPLEY John 175
SHORT Adam 64; Edward 34, 72; Jeremiah 81; Jerry 34; John 36
Sidney Park 192
Sidney Park farm 94
SIDWELL Levi 87
SILLETO Edward 28
SILLICK Nathaniel 121
SILLITOE Edward 79
Silvanus Folly 33
SILVER Amos 97, 143; Benjamin 93, 132, 156, 189, 202; David 96, 177; Gersham 97; James 97; Silas 111, 144, 169; William 111, 132, 164
SIMMONS Mrs. H. 176
SIMPER Richard 81
SIMPERS Henry G. 85; Jacob 43, 85; Jesse 36, 88; John E. 11; Johnson 5, 78; Richard 41, 82; Richard Jr 57; Thomas 43; Thomas sen 57; William 28, 41
SIMPSON Henry 36, 53; Mary 15, 53; Mrs. 49
SIMS J. B. 66; Joseph B. 13, 68
SINGLETON James 181

SINNOTT John 71
SKINNER Robert 34
SLADE Belinda 169; Dixon 127; John 106; Julia 133
Slade's Charm 127
SLEE J. 116; John 116, 136, 182, 191; Joseph 136, 191; Rev Joseph 182
SLICER Henry 134; John 13; Rev 117, 177; Thomas John 13
SLUYTER Benjamin 59; Benjamin T. 87
SMEDLEY Joel 90
SMITH ...nston D. 95; A. C. 31; Amos 121, 134; Andrew C. 40; Benjamin 79; Col. William 133; Cornelius 13, 16, 23; Daniel 127; David 190; Edward 134; Eli 177; Eliza 103; Elizabeth 79; Frances 181, 189; Francis 4, 60; George 190; Henry 109, 134, 179; Henry C. 96; Hugh jun 111; Hugh sen 111; Isaac W. 38; Isreal 30; James 95, 96, 106, 116, 133, 183; Jane 190; Jehu 102, 165, 208; John 28, 80, 103, 177; John W. 146; Joseph 96; Margaret 204; Mr. 16, 57; Paca 129, 199, 204; Reuben 111; Rev Thomas 56, 84, 91; Richard 144; Robert W. 142, 169; Samuel 169, 177, 183, 190; Samuel R. 98, 131; Sarah 209; W. D. 111; William 59, 63, 80, 90, 111, 199; William of Samuel 132, 177; Winston D. 132, 137, 151
Smith's Still 126
SMITHSON Edward 127; Elizabeth 195; Esther S. 195; John 115, 132, 177, 195; Luther 127; Mary 195; Renis 124; Thomas 195; Thomas of Nathaniel 177; William 106, 124, 169, 195
Smithville Woollen Cloth Factory 181
SNEDEN Rev 129
SNEED Ann Elizabeth 177; John T. 186
SNELL James 80
SNOW Frisby 92
SOLDEN Thomas 144
SOUTHERN Henry 10
SPENCE Miss Strena(?) 194
SPENCER John 28
Spencer's Meadow-ground 98
Spesutia narrows 192
SPICER Abraham 106; Alexander 124
SPRATT Samuel 36
SPRIGG Joseph 134
Spring Forest 189
SPRING Mary 46, 86
SPRINGER James 25, 46, 86; John 8; Samuel 28

SPRY Col. George 10
ST. CLAIR Alizanna 154; Ann 154; Elizabeth 116; George 154; James 154 Lester 154; Martha 154; Mary 154; Moses 160; William 154
St. Clair's Good Luck 154
STACKHOUSE William 23
Stafford Mills 102
Stage lines 108
STALCUP Andrew 17
STANDLEY Peregrine 50
STANLEY Abraham 195; Peregrine 5
STANSBURY Edward 173; Isaac 177
STANTON John 11, 13, 15, 17; Maria 17
STARK Edward Benedict 150; Eliza 150
STATEN Henry 79
Stedman's Delight 4
STEEL James 106, 132, 177
STEELE David 134
STEEN James, A.M. 187
STELLING William 36
STEPHENS Thomas 40, 41, 48
STEPHENSON James 124, 127, 166, 203; Rev William 157, 164; William B. 146
STERLING Ephraim 10
STERRETT & WALKER 16
STERRETT Lieut John S. 187
STEVENS B. H. 25; Benjamin H. 30; Jacob 53; Susan 33; Susanna 88; Thomas 33, 88; W. B. 71; William 84
STEVENSON Ezekiel 29; Rev 201
STEWART Benedict 175; Bennet 104; David 127; Henry 92; James Jr 54; Robert 133
STIDLAM Miss E. 34
STILES H. 25
STILLINGS James 108, 117, 152
STITES Henry S. 23; Major Henry S. 117
STOCKSON Richard C. 195
STOCKTON Joseph 18
STOKES David 111; Harvey 111, 116; John 111; Joseph of David 111
STONE John L. 79; Samuel 202
STONEY Charles 62
Stoney Ridge 190
STOOPS Augustus 72; Joseph 32
Story's Meadows 82
STRADLEY Thomas 28
Strawberry Hills 104
STREET Abraham of David 116; Col. John 125, 195; David 133; Glenn 106; Hanna 95; John 126, 185; Mary 206; Roger 132, 173, 183; Rogers 116, 133; Thomas of John 177; Thomas of Thomas 95, 169

STREETT Capt 149; John 103, 177; Mary 176
STREIGTHOOF Peter 172
STRICKER Jacob 25
Strife Angle 127
STROBLE Zacary 183
STU... William 95
STUMP & PARKER 102
STUMP ___ 79; H. 2; Harrison 100; Henry 40,. 67, 93, 111; Herman 111; J. W. 127; John 5, 52, 86, 94, 98, 127, 150; John W. 94, 98, 106, 150, 169; Rachel 52; Reuben 93; Samuel 111; Thomas C. 132, 177; William 111, 133; William H. 127; William Herman 192
Stump's Old fields 93
STUPS Gustin 28
STURGEON James 74; Thomas 31, 74
SUEZENIER Robert 96
SUGARS Francis 30
SULLIVAN Sarah P. 14, 59; William 111
SUTHERLAND Alexander 150
SUTTON Elizabeth 33; Joel 56; Jonathan 101; Samuel 194; Samuell 169; Thomas 62
SWAGGERT John 41
Swampy Point 208
SWARTZ Ephraim 206
SWEARINGEN Sheriff 163
SYKES Dr. James 28; Sarah 195

TAGART John 136
TALLEY Jane 74
TARMAN James 160; Rhoda 160
TARRING Henry 134
TATMAN Collins 2, 51
TAYLOR Abner 30; Ann 79; Capt 70; Daniel 95; Edmun 59; Isaac 9; Jacob M. 9, 22; James of William 170; Jeremiah 9, 18; John 42; John S. 86; Robert 127, 166; Samuel 30, 42; Thomas 25; William 37, 78
Taylor's Mount 155
TAYSON Elysha 169
TEALAR John 36
TEASE Alexander 106
TEMPLE William 116, 168
TERRY Hozea 19, 89
TEZIN James 144
THOMAS A. J. 51, 94; Ann 15, 53, 79; Ann E. 56; C. A. 25; Eleanor 22; George 80; George W. 4; Haret 36; J. W. 25; James 59; Jesse 7; John H. 91; John W. 12, 32; Joseph 31; Joseph Jr 5; Lavinea 92; Lewis 23; Mordecai 111; Rebecca 62; Samuel 2, 15, 50, 62; Sarah 13; Theodore 11, 15, 20, 22; Thomas S. 5, 51, 79, 92; William 59, 62, 79, 120, 123
Thomas Fishery 63
THOMPSON ___ 52; Aquilla 133; James 10; John 36; John of Thomas, sr 169; Josias 95; Martha 133; Mary A. 62; Rev 84; Thomas 95; William 10, 92
Thompson's Fortune 165
Three Sisters 140
TIBBITT Samuel 34
TILDEN Catharine 83; Lieut Thomas B. 62
TILGHMAN Henry 57
TILLOTSON Abraham 53. 59; Dr. Abraham 37, 42
TODD Levi 79
TOLAND Adam 143; Benjamin 95; Benjamin Jr 143
Toland's Reserve 143
TOLLEY James W. 132
TORBERT William Jr 91
TORBORT Andrew 111
TOUCHSTONE Henry 114
TOWNSAND William M. 15
TOWNSEND Dr. G. S. 4; Dr. Granville S. 12; Joseph 14, 69
TREDWAY John 106; Thomas 124, 133, 169
TREDWELL James 169
TREMBLE Mr. 34
Triple Union 101
TROUTNER David 111
TRUMP Michael 34, 87
TUCKER William 120, 123
TUMBLIN Martha 53
TUPLI Ulrick 95
TURK Andrew 105
Turkey Range 170
TURNER George 66, 86; George C. 6; George H. 30; John P. 80; Sarah 6
TYLOR William 1
TYSON Emsen 34; Isaac 1, 161; Jacob 4; Joseph 29; Mary 29; Mathias 45. 92; Nathan 29; Samuel 23; Thomas 45; William 53

UNDERHILL Dann 80
UNDERWOOD Rachel 79
Union Fishery 98
USILTON Joseph 62

VAIL Thomas 8, 39, 56
VALENTINE family 151
VALENTINE James 34
VALINGTINE James 15
VANCE Elizabeth 171; James 36; Sarah 34; William 132; William C. 124
VANDEGRIFT Nicholas 25, 69
VANDEVER Margaret 36
VANSANT Wiliam 137
VAUGHAN John C. 106
VEACH Margaret 7
VEAZEY Benoni 3; Col. 18; Dave E. 34; Rachel 59; Thomas W. 42
VEAZY Thomas W. 87
VINK William 106
VIRTUE & HOGG 45
VIRTUE John 63; Mr. 2; Robert 17, 18
VOGDES Sarah 30, 92
VOSBURY Levi 30

W... John 135
WA... Daniel 169
WADE Ann 198
WADLOW Solomon 106
WAFTERS William 139
WAGGONER Joseph 58; Mrs. 32, 88
WAGNER Mary 79; Mrs. 203; Thomas 9
WAITES James 59
WAKELAND John 111
WALKER David 59; Elizabeth 1, 46; James 190; John 59; Samuel 15
WALL Mr. 16
WALLACE Dr. George 17; Elizabeth 53; Frisby 6; James 1, 62, 178; James B. 17; Rachael 75; Sarah 92; William 111
Wallace's Good Design 17
WALLASTON Mary 6, 65
WALLER George 79
WALLIS Hugh 81; John 121; Joseph 111
WALLON Jacob 25
WALMSLEY Margaret 36
WALTHAM Charlton 118; Charlton M. 177'; Hester 118; Susan E. 62
WALTON Nathan 150, 169, 183
WANN Daniel 132, 133; John 195; Susanna 211
WAPLES Gideon 91
War of 1812 (Desripction of Battle of Baltimore) 121
WARBURTON Thomas 87
WARD Charles 111; James 160; Jane 116; John 41, 111, 183; John S. 121, 172; Joseph 183; Peregrine 33; Perry 79, 92; Rachel 160; Rebecca 29; Richard 111; Thomas 195; William 34, 59, 125; William H. 5
WARDAN William 111
WARDEN Dr. James 16
WAREHAM George 132; Matilda 207
WARNER Aseph 149; Asoph 111; Jonathan 169, 178, 195; Joseph 111; Joseph E. 106; Silas 111; Thomas 111; William H. 96; William W. 101
WARNICK William 53, 92
WARNUK William 79
WARREN Henry 104
WARTER Benedict F. 96
WARTHON Elias 170
WARUM Abraham 28
Washington Hotel 43
WATERMAN Vintentia 95
WATERS Amos 114, 132, 187; Benjamin 114; Henry G. 132; J. P. 133; John 101; Lynix 92; Mary 116; Stephen 101, 132
WATERSON William 106
WATKINS Abel 132; John 124; Joseph 9; Mary Ann 194; Mouson 89; Mrs. 194; Samuel 134, 135
WATON John 15
WATSON James 101; John 87; William 111
WATT William 116
WATTERS Amos 177; Esther 174; Henry G. 177, 202, 211; John 174; Sally 101; Stephen 177, 196
Watters Meeting House 202
WAY Samuel 111
Weather conditions 84, 104, 127, 143
WEAVER Jonathan 53
WEBB Samuel 206; William 48
WEBBERTS John 79
WEBSTER Henry 143, 183, 194; John 99; John S. 192; Martha 195; Richard 185; William W. 99, 211
WEEMS Mr. 61
WEISER Lydia 106
Welch Point 69
WELCH William P. 116
WELLS and MAHAN 40
WELLS Benjamin N. 195; James 111; Orin 25; Penelope 35
WELSH & HARDING 38
Welsh Point 25
WESLEY March 34
WEST Mahlon 132; Mahlon H. 110, 141; Stacy 201; Susan 201; Thomas 96
WETHERAL James 132
WETHERALL James 120, 123

WHAN Adam 40; Adam, P.M. 53
WHANN Adam 8, 15; A., P.M. 34; Adam, P.M. 28, 36, 59, 79, 92; James 106; John 72; Mary Ann 106; Nathaniel 106; Samuel 106
WHEELER Elizabeth 195; Francis J. 102; George M. 167, 187; Ja... 95; James B. 167; Joseph 171; Rebecca 167; Richard J. 102; Teresa 147
Wheeler's & Clark's Contrivance 102
WHERRY Eben'zr 11; John D. 92
Whetstone Point 144
WHITAKER James 116, 124; Joshua 165, 195; Platt 177; Samuel 177
WHITE David 3, 39; Easter 79; Ester 92; Israel 6, 45; James 94; Margaret 8; Thomas 13, 14, 25, 34
White House 4, 179
WHITEFORD Cungm. 111; Daniel 111; Hugh 111; Hugh of M. 111; Hugh of W. 111; Michael 111, 132; William 111
WHITEHEAD Thomas 183
WHITELOCK William 92
WHITHAM William 6
WHITSON Joseph 106
WHITTAKER Platt 132
WHITTEMORE Henry 188
Whortleberry Hills 209
WICKES Ann 62; Antonietta 62
Widow's Garden 102
WIGDON Major 5
WIGGINS John 111; Thomas 111
WIGTON Major 46
WILCOX Joseph 36
Wild Cat Den 101
WILE Joshua 139
WILES Aquila 167; Joshua 139
WILEY John 132; Mary 124; Matthew 124; Nathaniel 59
WILKINS Milcah 91
WILKINSON N. 28
William's Discovery 129, 182
WILLIAMS Abigail 164; Averilla 62; Capt James 96; Grace 164; Jacob 11, 87; James 164; James W. 77, 99, 111, 121, 123; John 36; Lloyd 195; Nathaniel 25; Thomas 85; William 35
Williams' Fortune 165
WILLIAMSON Jane 34; Jesse 111; John 36, 59, 111; Rev 69; Rev Moses 92; Samuel 92; Thomas 111
WILLSON Isaac T. 164
WILSON ___ 182; Alexander 7, 40; Andrew 183; Archibald 169; Christopher 111, 183, 205; Chrs. sen 111; Colonel Thomas 84; Edward 9, 11, 17, 32, 72; George H. 124, 177, 189; H. 132; Isaac 2, 41, 52, 97, 99, 104, 111; Isaac T. 108, 169; James 108, 111, 132, 177; John 2, 52, 74, 79, 92, 100, 177; John of William 189; Joshua 119, 121; Josias 106, 116; Letitia 116; Mary 7, 36; Mr. 137; Philip 13; Philip Jr 13; Priscilla 171; Samuel 11, 15, 45, 49; Susan 156; Thomas 101, 104, 211; Washington 45; William 97, 100, 156, 177, 195; William H. 15, 16, 116
WINGATE & MANLY 68, 84
WINGATE Edward 6, 18; Henry 64; John 7, 19; Mr. 14; Nicholas 64; Robert 19; W. 7, 13, 72; William 6, 18, 19, 33, 46, 63
WIRT John T. 53; John W. 29
WODSWORTH Lydia 169
WOLF Mr. 5
WOLFE Nathaniel 36
WOLMSLEY Rachel 71
WOOD Avid 150; John 200
WOODALL William 35
WOODLAND John 183
WOODLEY Cottage 134
WOODROW Josiah 46; Stephen 19
Woods Close 178
WOODS David 150; John 150
Woolen Factory 9
WOOLFORD Capt Arthur 164; Capt Hiram 16; Rev 75; Stevens W. 20, 22
WOOLSEY ___ 185; George 130; Henry 97, 195; William 101, 130
WORDSWORTH John 194
WORK Mary 59; Rachel 28
WORRELL Grace 15; Mrs. 51; Thomas Jr 92; William P. 83
Worsell Manor 38
WORTH James 34
WORTHINGTON Dr. Thomas 176; Hannah R. 157; John 105; Joseph 132, 177; Priscilla 178; Samuel 111; William 108, 5, 111; Zenas 5
WRIGHT Caleb 124; John 111; John of Thomas 111; Major Edward 51; Mark 111; Thomas 111; William 34
WROTH John 1, 2, 9, 43, 87
WYLE Joshua 95

YATES Evan D. 11, 63; Mr. 5
YEARLY Nathan 101
Yellot's Mill 105

-80-

YELLOTT Rebecca R. 178
YORK Diana 53
Yorkshire 63
YOUNG John 201
Young Man's addition 192

Zebulon's Fancy 17

Index of Single names
Following are names for which no surname is given. In most cases these are slaves.

Abraham 28, 99
Ann 101, 104
Betsey 107
Bil 100
Bob 203
Catherine 28
Charles 99, 198, 203
Cope 100
Delia 101
Dinah 203
Eliza 180
George 28, 99
Gerard 107
Grace 165
Hager 99
Hampton 100
Hariet 102
Harriet 203
Harry 101
Hellen 101
Henry 32, 99
Isaac 28
Jack 100
Jacob 28, 78, 145
Jane 28, 147
Jim 100
Jinny 104
Joe 203
John 25, 28
Josh 202
Julia 142
Julian 101, 147
Lewis 100, 159
Lucy 165
Margaret 28
Mariah 101
Mariam 202
Mary 206
Mifflin 95

Milly 170
Montgomery 19
Morin 19
Nace 100
Nancy 211
Ned 165
Nelly 101
Parker 159
Patrick 32
Patty 211
Peter 202
Phil 100
Philip 203
Poll 99
Rosetta 97
Sam 28, 100, 101
Sarah 104
Spencer 99
Stephen 106
Stokes 102
Susan 100, 101, 104
Thomas 78
William 28

Other books by F. Edward Wright:

Abstracts of Bucks County, Pennsylvania Wills, 1685-1785
Abstracts of Cumberland County, Pennsylvania Wills, 1750-1785
Abstracts of Cumberland County, Pennsylvania Wills, 1785-1825
Abstracts of Philadelphia County Wills, 1726-1747
Abstracts of Philadelphia County Wills, 1748-1763
Abstracts of Philadelphia County Wills, 1763-1784
Abstracts of Philadelphia County Wills, 1777-1790
Abstracts of Philadelphia County Wills, 1790-1802
Abstracts of Philadelphia County Wills, 1802-1809
Abstracts of Philadelphia County Wills, 1810-1815
Abstracts of Philadelphia County Wills, 1815-1819
Abstracts of Philadelphia County Wills, 1820-1825
Abstracts of Philadelphia County, Pennsylvania Wills, 1682-1726
Abstracts of South Central Pennsylvania Newspapers, Volume 1, 1785-1790
Abstracts of South Central Pennsylvania Newspapers, Volume 3, 1796-1800
Abstracts of the Newspapers of Georgetown and the Federal City, 1789-99
Abstracts of York County, Pennsylvania Wills, 1749-1819
Bucks County, Pennsylvania Church Records of the 17th and 18th Centuries Volume 2: Quaker Records: Falls and Middletown Monthly Meetings
Anna Miller Watring and F. Edward Wright
Caroline County, Maryland Marriages, Births and Deaths, 1850-1880
Citizens of the Eastern Shore of Maryland, 1659-1750
Cumberland County, Pennsylvania Church Records of the 18th Century
Delaware Newspaper Abstracts, Volume 1: 1786-1795
Early Charles County, Maryland Settlers, 1658-1745
Marlene Strawser Bates and F. Edward Wright
Early Church Records of Alexandria City and Fairfax County, Virginia
F. Edward Wright and Wesley E. Pippenger
Early Church Records of New Castle County, Delaware, Volume 1, 1701-1800
Frederick County Militia in the War of 1812
Sallie A. Mallick and F. Edward Wright
Inhabitants of Baltimore County, 1692-1763
Land Records of Sussex County, Delaware, 1769-1782
Land Records of Sussex County, Delaware, 1782-1789
Elaine Hastings Mason and F. Edward Wright
Marriage Licenses of Washington, District of Columbia, 1811-1830
Marriages and Deaths from the Newspapers of Allegany and Washington Counties, Maryland, 1820-1830
Marriages and Deaths from The York Recorder, 1821-1830
Marriages and Deaths in the Newspapers of Frederick and Montgomery Counties, Maryland, 1820-1830

Marriages and Deaths in the Newspapers of Lancaster County, Pennsylvania, 1821-1830
Marriages and Deaths in the Newspapers of Lancaster County, Pennsylvania, 1831-1840
Marriages and Deaths of Cumberland County, [Pennsylvania], 1821-1830
Maryland Calendar of Wills Volume 9: 1744-1749
Maryland Calendar of Wills Volume 10: 1748-1753
Maryland Calendar of Wills Volume 11: 1753-1760
Maryland Calendar of Wills Volume 12: 1759-1764
Maryland Calendar of Wills Volume 13: 1764-1767
Maryland Calendar of Wills Volume 14: 1767-1772
Maryland Calendar of Wills Volume 15: 1772-1774
Maryland Calendar of Wills Volume 16: 1774-1777
Maryland Eastern Shore Newspaper Abstracts, Volume 1: 1790-1805
Maryland Eastern Shore Newspaper Abstracts, Volume 2: 1806-1812
Maryland Eastern Shore Newspaper Abstracts, Volume 3: 1813-1818
Maryland Eastern Shore Newspaper Abstracts, Volume 4: 1819-1824
Maryland Eastern Shore Newspaper Abstracts, Volume 5: Northern Counties, 1825-1829
F. Edward Wright and Irma Harper
Maryland Eastern Shore Newspaper Abstracts, Volume 6: Southern Counties, 1825-1829
Maryland Eastern Shore Newspaper Abstracts, Volume 7: Northern Counties, 1830-1834
Irma Harper and F. Edward Wright
Maryland Eastern Shore Newspaper Abstracts, Volume 8: Southern Counties, 1830-1834
Maryland Militia in the Revolutionary War
S. Eugene Clements and F. Edward Wright
Newspaper Abstracts of Allegany and Washington Counties, Maryland, 1811-1815
Newspaper Abstracts of Cecil and Harford Counties, Maryland, 1822-1830
Newspaper Abstracts of Frederick County, Maryland, 1816-1819
Newspaper Abstracts of Frederick County, Maryland, 1811-1815
Sketches of Maryland Eastern Shoremen
Tax List of Chester County, Pennsylvania 1768
Tax List of York County, Pennsylvania 1779
Washington County Church Records of the 18th Century, 1768-1800
Western Maryland Newspaper Abstracts, Volume 1: 1786-1798
Western Maryland Newspaper Abstracts, Volume 2: 1799-1805
Western Maryland Newspaper Abstracts, Volume 3: 1806-1810
Wills of Chester County, Pennsylvania, 1766-1778

www.ingramcontent.com/pod-product-compliance
Lightning Source LLC
Chambersburg PA
CBHW061501040426
42450CB00008B/1439